IDHA APAM VIJASAITI

VANGHUHI DAENA ASHEM VOHU

VISPAISH AVI KARSHVAN

"Henceforth from now may spread
ASHA, the best of all things
Over all the eight spheres."

Zarathustra, Avesta, Yasht 13—94

THIS BOOK IS DEDICATED
TO ALL AT THE GRAND CENTRAL STATION
OF THE TWENTIETH CENTURY
WHO ARE LONGING FOR OUR LOST SYMBIOSIS
OF THOUSANDS OF YEARS
WITH NATURE, SIMPLICITY AND PEACE.

THE
ESSENE
BOOK OF ASHA

Journey to the Cosmic Ocean

by
EDMOND BORDEAUX SZEKELY

MCMLXXXIX
INTERNATIONAL BIOGENIC SOCIETY

SOME BOOKS BY EDMOND BORDEAUX SZEKELY

THE ESSENE WAY—BIOGENIC LIVING
THE ESSENE GOSPEL OF PEACE, BOOK ONE
BOOK TWO, THE UNKNOWN BOOKS OF THE ESSENES
BOOK THREE, LOST SCROLLS OF THE ESSENE BROTHERHOOD
BOOK FOUR, THE TEACHINGS OF THE ELECT
THE DISCOVERY OF THE ESSENE GOSPEL: The Essenes and the Vatican
SEARCH FOR THE AGELESS, in Three Volumes
THE ESSENE BOOK OF CREATION
THE ESSENE JESUS
THE ESSENE BOOK OF ASHA
THE ZEND AVESTA OF ZARATHUSTRA
ARCHEOSOPHY, A NEW SCIENCE
THE ESSENE ORIGINS OF CHRISTIANITY
TEACHINGS OF THE ESSENES FROM ENOCH TO THE DEAD SEA SCROLLS
THE ESSENES, BY JOSEPHUS AND HIS CONTEMPORARIES
THE ESSENE TEACHINGS OF ZARATHUSTRA
THE ESSENE SCIENCE OF LIFE
THE ESSENE CODE OF LIFE
THE ESSENE SCIENCE OF FASTING AND THE ART OF SOBRIETY
ESSENE COMMUNIONS WITH THE INFINITE
THE FIRST ESSENE
THE BIOGENIC REVOLUTION
THE ORIGIN OF LIFE
THE COSMOTHERAPY OF THE ESSENES
THE LIVING BUDDHA
MAN IN THE COSMIC OCEAN
TOWARD THE CONQUEST OF THE INNER COSMOS
FATHER, GIVE US ANOTHER CHANCE
THE ECOLOGICAL HEALTH GARDEN, THE BOOK OF SURVIVAL
THE TENDER TOUCH: BIOGENIC FULFILLMENT
THE DIALECTICAL METHOD OF THINKING
THE EVOLUTION OF HUMAN THOUGHT
THE SOUL OF ANCIENT MEXICO
THE NEW FIRE
ANCIENT AMERICA: PARADISE LOST
PILGRIM OF THE HIMALAYAS
MESSENGERS FROM ANCIENT CIVILIZATIONS
SEXUAL HARMONY and the Art of Raising Happy, Healthy Children
LUDWIG VAN BEETHOVEN, PROMETHEUS OF THE MODERN WORLD
THE FIERY CHARIOTS
CREATIVE WORK: KARMA YOGA
THE ART OF STUDY: THE SORBONNE METHOD
COSMOS, MAN AND SOCIETY
THE BOOK OF LIVING FOODS
SCIENTIFIC VEGETARIANISM
THE CONQUEST OF DEATH

Book Design by Golondrina Graphics

Editor's Preface to the 1989 Edition

The Art of Asha: Journey to the Cosmic Ocean was the first book of Edmond Bordeaux Szekely that I helped to prepare for publication. Carrying out the various tasks assigned to me by the author, I poured my young heart and soul into my contribution to the book, feeling there could be no greater honor than to be part of this magnificent presentation of the Art of Asha. Almost 23 years later, I feel the same thrill of creative energy and an even deeper gratitude for the privilege of bringing this new edition to life.

In the years between 1966, when *The Art of Asha* was first published, and 1979, when Edmond Bordeaux Szekely died, his interpretation of Zarathustrian cosmology and cosmogony underwent a profound transformation. He had always spoken of the Art of Asha as the spiritual ancestor of the Essene Tree of Life; and in his lectures he often emphasized the importance of studying the Art of Asha as a foundation for true understanding of the Essene philosophy. But in his last years, at his Seminars and in his writing, he gave greater and greater importance to the teachings of Zarathustra, not only as a basis of study of other great World Pictures, but as the very keystone, the central point, the most vital and important of all spiritual revelations of history. He often said that "intelligence is the ability to adapt ourselves adequately to unexpected changes in the environment," and as the seventies drew to a close he concluded that a thorough knowledge and *active* use of the Art of Asha was the most effective method of dealing with those unexpected changes.

"Unexpected changes" was a rather optimistic way of describing the problems of the world, problems which have multiplied dramatically since 1979: the pressing urgency of world famine, starvation, unemployment, substandard living conditions, homelessness, increasing crime and terrorism, violence and wars, intolerance and violation of human rights, the terrible depletion of our natural resources, accumulation of nuclear waste, and even the threat of total environmental destruction. He felt strongly that what was needed most to solve these urgent problems was a philosophy of life that would challenge us to immediate action; one that would stimulate us to be active points in the universe, declaring ourselves firmly on the side of Light and Good in all things. And the Art of Asha, in all its aspects—including a form of self-analysis that places us directly in the arena of struggle to maintain and preserve Life in the face of all that threatens it—is the most important philosophy we can master.

With this urgency in mind, he revised *The Essene Book of Asha* (as he re-named it in 1976, in order to emphasize the unbroken lineage between all the great World Pictures of history), and it is from his notes that I have edited this present version. The only real difference between this and earlier editions is the later emphasis on ASHA as the *direct* experience of life as the outcome of the battle of opposing forces, rather than simply a fascinating distant ancestor of Chess. Present-day Chess is a pastime, something to be enjoyed apart from the real activities of daily life. But the Art of Asha *is* Life, and in learning the Art of Asha, we learn how to live in the truest sense of the word: how to absorb ever-increasing energy, harmony and knowledge from the natural and cosmic forces permanently flowing in and around us, and so further our own individual evolution and that of our planet. In the words of Romain Rolland, "let us put aside everything which divides us, and concentrate on all the things which unite us. Let us mobilize all the forces of Life against the forces of death."

—Norma Nilsson Bordeaux Szekely

January 1, 1989.

CONTENTS

Scattered throughout the volume are illustrations of archeological representations of ancient Zarathustrian symbols from Sumeria, Persia, India, China, Babylonia, Tibet, Phoenicia, etc.

INTRODUCTION

From the remote ages of antiquity a remarkable teaching has existed which is universal in its application and ageless in its wisdom. Fragments of it are found in Sumerian hieroglyphs and on tiles and stones dating back some eight or ten thousand years. Some of the symbols, such as for the sun, moon, air, water and other natural forces, are from an even earlier age preceding the cataclysm that ended the Pleistocene period. How many thousands of years previous to that the teaching existed is unknown.

These teachings permeated the stream of traditions to which the Hebrew people were exposed in the Babylonian prison, dating from the Gilgamesh Epics to the Zend Avesta of Zarathustra. Echoes of it were also found in the stream of traditions flowing with poetical majesty through the Old and New Testaments, dating from the ageless Enoch and the other Patriarchs, through the Prophets and on to the mysterious Essene Brotherhood, which flourished during the last two or three centuries B.C. and the first century of the Christian era at the Dead Sea in Palestine and at Lake Mareotis in Egypt.

In the buried library of the Essene Brotherhood at the Dead Sea, where the greatest number of scrolls were found, the texts of these two streams of traditions were very much interwoven. They follow each other in a strange succession: the powerful cubistic simplicity of the first juxtaposed with the majestic, expressionist poetry of the second.

In the Art of Asha, with its drama of light and darkness, the interplay of forces of good and evil, we experience the power of the Avestic tradition. In the Essene Tree of Life, with the branches of man reaching toward the Heavenly Father, and the roots of man sunk deep into the Earthly Mother, the symbolism of the Biblical Patriarchs is revealed. Both the Art of Asha and the Essene Tree of Life are reflections of the same truth: in his quest for perfection, man is always guided by the visible forces of nature and the invisible forces of the cosmos.

Zarathustra and the Zend Avesta

THE LEGEND OF ZARATHUSTRA

In Maeterlinck's little masterpiece, *The Blue Bird,* the two children, Tyltyl and Mytyl, seek the bird—the symbol of happiness throughout creation, but after the most fantastic adventures awake to find it in their own home.

The story symbolizes the quest of humanity for thousands of years and through all ages of history. Pursuing happiness, mankind has gone through all possible experiences. On the path it has trodden in its evolution lie all manner of social systems, customs, and civilizations.

Zarathustra's basic attitude is eternal vigilance as the price of vitality, happiness and wisdom. This is not the fatalistic outlook of the Mohammedan whereby everything is written in advance, so that it is useless to try to change it. Nor is it the attitude of depreciation of the things of this world in the hope of future life, which distinguished medieval Christianity with its doctrine that the present life is but a mournful antechamber to the true life that is to come. Nor again is it the philosophic withdrawal from the chaos of the world found in Buddhism or the teachings of the Hindu sages, to whom the world is mere appearance, without value. Nor, lastly, is it the attitude of superficiality and indifference shown by modern man in the face of the great problems of life. Zarathustra adopts a dynamic attitude of eternal vigilance, which will prevent even the appearance of evil, and, if evil has crept in, will fight and destroy it. The follower of Zarathustra knew that this was a heroic and lifelong task, since the forces of evil have great power in ourselves, in society, on the planet and throughout the universe. But he also knew that in this glorious and unceasing struggle he had at his disposal a great arsenal in the shape of all the sources of energy, harmony and knowledge to be found in mankind, nature and the cosmos.

If we examine the world situation today we find that mankind is still following that same eternal purpose, but is no nearer to its achievement. From the countries of every continent comes news every hour of the day of wars, disorder, famine, injustice, persecution, hatred, destruction of age-old values, ignorance and selfishness. All are symptoms of the general chaos which afflicts the contemporary world. Like Maeterlinck's two children, humanity still does not realize that it has the Blue Bird within its grasp—that it has had it for thousands of years.

The Blue Bird came to humanity when it received that first and greatest encyclopedia—the Zend Avesta of Zarathustra. This every-sided and eternally valid teaching is as yet undiscovered, because humanity does not know that it possesses it. And through its very simplicity and clarity it is difficult to find. Yet now as never before mankind has need of the message of the Avesta, which I want to present in the most vivid way, in the form of the oldest Parsee legend, *The Legend of Zarathustra*.

Once, long ago, when Vishtaspa, king of Persia, was returning from a victorious campaign, he came near to the place where Zarathustra lived and taught his disciples. He decided to visit the famous man, whose name was known to every Persian, and to see if he could answer those difficult questions which the wise men in his palace were unable to explain.

The king and his retinue turned aside to Zarathustra's place and saw a man who seemed to be a teacher, with a group of disciples around him. All were busy in an orchard, and the Master appeared to be instructing them. At the king's approach the disciples withdrew.

Then the king said to Zarathustra: "I believe you to be the great Zarathustra and I have come that you may explain to me the laws of nature and the universe. If you are as wise a man as my people declare, this will doubtless not take you long. I cannot tarry, as I am on my way home from a war and important matters of state await me at my palace."

Looking at the king, Zarathustra took a grain of wheat from the earth and gave it to him. "In this small grain of wheat," he declared, "are contained all the laws of the universe and the forces of nature." The king was much astonished by this answer, which he did not understand. And when he saw smiles on the faces of those around him, he was angry and threw the grain upon the ground, thinking that he was being mocked. And to Zarathustra he said: "I believed that you were a wise man and a great philosopher, but I now see that you are a stubborn and ignorant man, hiding your ignorance beneath the cloak of exaggeration. I was foolish to waste my time by coming here to see you." And with that the king turned to depart and rode on to his palace.

Then Zarathustra picked up the grain, saying to his disciples: "I will keep this grain of wheat, because it will one day be needed by the king and will be his teacher."

The years passed. The king was successful as ruler and warrior, and led a life of luxury and apparent contentment in his palace. But at night, when he went to bed, strange thoughts came into his mind and troubled him.

"I live in luxury and abundance in this splendid palace," thought the king, "but not far away are multitudes of people who live in misery and want, who are cold and are hungry. Why am I king? Why do I have power over all men and all things in my empire? Why are the people poor and why do they suffer? How long shall I enjoy this abundance and power, and what will happen to me when I die? Can my power and my riches save me from illness and death? What will they avail when I lie in my grave? What will happen when my body turns to dust and feeds the worms? Will aught be left of this life or is everything lost with the coming of death? If I pass on to another life, shall I still be myself, or shall I be someone entirely different? And if there is another life, what shall I experience in it? Shall I continue to have the power and riches of my present life, or shall I be a vagabond with no place to lay my head, exposed to all the inclemency of nature and lacking money for the morrow's food? What happened before I came into this life? Did I live before in this country or in another? Or was I born for the first time into this life? How did life begin? How did the world come into being, and what was there before life appeared? What was there before the creation of the universe? Was the universe created by someone, and was that someone God? Who created God? What is time? What existed before time? Does eternity exist? If so, how can we conceive eternity?"

The nights of the king were tormented by such questions, and often he did not sleep till morning came.

No one in the palace could answer these questions, but meanwhile the fame of Zarathustra grew. The king was aware that many disciples were coming to the teacher from many lands, and he felt that there was the man who might be able to tell him more of these problems than anyone else. So putting by his pride, he dispatched a great caravan of treasure to Zarathustra and with it an invitation and a request. "I regret," he wrote, "that when I was impatient and thoughtless in my youth, I asked you to explain the great problems of existence in a few minutes of time. I have changed and do not want the impossible. But I am still deeply interested to know the laws of the universe and the forces of nature, even more so than when I was a young man. Come to my palace, I pray you, or if that is not possible, send to me the best of your disciples that he may teach me all he can about these questions."

After an interval the caravan and the messengers returned. These told the king that they had found Zarathustra, who sent him greeting but returned the proffered treasure. The treasure, Zarathustra had said, was of no use to a gardener, but he was glad to keep the wrappings of the packages, as they would be useful to protect his trees and plants against the cold of winter. Moreover Zarathustra had sent the king a gift wrapped in a leaf and had asked the messengers to tell him that this was the teacher who would teach him everything concerning the forces of nature and the laws of the universe. "I am not sending one of my disciples," Zarathustra had said, "but my own teacher who has taught me all I know about the laws of life. I trust that the king will be as apt to learn as my teacher is to teach."

Then the king asked where the teacher was and in reply the messengers handed him the little gift wrapped in the leaf. The king opened it and found the same grain of wheat that Zarathustra had given him before. He was greatly perturbed by the wheat and thought there must be something mysterious and magical in it. So he put it in a golden box and hid it among his treasures. Almost every day he looked at it, expecting some miracle to happen, such as the turning of the grain of wheat into something or someone that would teach him all he wished to know.

Months went by, but nothing happened. At last the king lost patience and said: "It seems that Zarathustra has deceived me again. Either he is making a mock of me or else he does not know the answers to my questions. I will show him that I can find the answers without his help." So the king sent a caravan to the great Indian philosopher

Tshengregacha, to whom came disciples from all parts of the world, and with the caravan went the same messengers and the same magnificent treasure that he had once sent to Zarathustra.

After many months the messengers returned from India and announced that the philosopher had consented to become the king's teacher and would soon arrive at his court. Then the king was glad and ordered that festivities be held in honor of his guest and, when the philosopher arrived, he thanked him for coming from such a far country.

But Tshengregacha said to him: "I am honored to be your teacher, but in frankness must tell you that I come chiefly to your country that I may meet the great Zarathustra, of whom I have heard such wide report. Indeed I do not know why you should have need of me when you are so near to one who can doubtless tell you more than I." Then the king took the golden box containing the grain of wheat and answered: "I asked Zarathustra to teach me; see, this is what he sent me. Here is the teacher who shall teach me the laws of the universe and the forces of nature. Is this not ridiculous? How can as great a teacher as you think Zarathustra to be commit such folly?"

Tshengregacha looked long at the grain of wheat and silence fell upon the palace while he meditated. At length he said: "I do not regret my many months of journeying, for now I know that Zarathustra is in truth the great teacher that I have long believed him to be. This tiny grain of wheat can indeed teach us the laws of the universe and the forces of nature, for it contains them in itself. Even as you must not keep the grain of wheat in its golden box if you would learn the answers to the weighty questions which trouble you and if you would grow in wisdom and understanding, so you yourself must not stay in this luxurious palace. If you plant this little grain in the earth where it belongs, in contact with the soil, the rain, the air, the sunshine and the light of the moon and of the stars, then, like a universe in itself, it will begin to grow bigger and bigger. Likewise you, if you would grow in knowledge and understanding, must leave this artificial palace and go into your garden, where you will be close to all the forces of nature and of the universe—to the sum total of things. Just as inexhaustible sources of energy are ever flowing towards the grain planted in the earth, so will innumerable sources of knowledge open and flow towards you, till you become one with nature and the organic universe. If you watch the growth of this seed of grain you will find that there is an indestructible and mysterious power in it—the power of life. If you watch long enough, you will see that the grain disappears and is replaced by a plant which will triumph over all obstacles and opposition—which will grow higher and higher and higher because it has life within it. If you throw a stone upwards, it falls again to the ground, since it is dead and not living and has not the mysterious power of life which enables the plant to grow higher and higher and to triumph over death. At the moment when the grain sprouts, and indeed at every instant of the plants' growth toward the Sun, there is victory over death."

"All that you say is true," answered the king, "yet in the end the plant will wither and die and will be dissolved in the earth."

"But not," said the philosopher, "until it has performed an act of creation and has turned itself into hundreds of grains each like the first. The tiny grain disappeared as it grew into a plant, and you, too, as you grow, must turn yourself into something and someone else. In the same way a great truth also seems to disappear and be turned into something that is seemingly different, but only to return in a greater form, like the hundred grains that take

15

the place of the one.

"You, too, must one day cease to be your present self, so that you may become a richer personality, in pursuance of the law that life always creates more life, truth more abundant truth, the seed more abundant seeds. This is one answer to your problems given by the grain of wheat. It teaches that everything is in movement and is constantly changing and growing; that life and all things else are the result of struggle between two opposite forces. If you go into your garden and will look at soil and rain, at the sky and the sun and the stars, they will teach you many more truths of a like kind.

"The grain of wheat is indeed a great teacher. We should be thankful to Zarathustra for having sent it to us. I propose that now we go to rest and that on the morrow we journey to Zarathustra himself that he may teach us more of these things. He will be able to tell you all that you wish to know of the matters which trouble you, and I myself will profit from his wisdom."

The king was much moved by Tshengregacha's words and readily agreed to his suggestion. In a few days' time they came to the garden of Zarathustra and understood at once the method by which he taught his disciples. His only book was the great book of nature, and he taught his disciples to read in it.

The two visitors learned another great truth in Zarathustra's garden: that life and work, study and leisure, are one and the same; that the right way to live is a simple, natural life—a creative life within which individual growth is a single total dynamic force. They spent a year in the garden, learning to read the laws of existence and of Life from the vast book of nature. At the end of that time the king returned to his own city and asked Zarathustra to set out systematically the essence of his great teaching. Zarathustra did so, and the result was the sacred book of the *Zend Avesta*, which by the king's command became the official religion of the Persian empire. Meanwhile Tshengregacha went back to India and there, being a poet as well as philosopher, he summed up all that he had learnt in Zarathustra's garden in the beautiful hymns of the *Rig-Veda*, another of the great sacred books of the East.

Persia became a great nation, growing ever more powerful as long as it followed Zarathustra's teaching in all its depth and simplicity, and as long as its people lived simple, natural and creative lives in accordance with the teaching of the *Avesta*. And when, like all imperial powers, the Persians departed from their simple, patriarchal way of life, becoming lazy from excess of wealth and might, they fell before the arms of a rising warrior nation, whose strength derived from the same purity and simplicity of life which had once formed the basis of the Persian power. Such is the cycle constantly recurring throughout universal history. The fate of the individual or of the nation will always be determined by the degree of his or its harmony with the forces of nature, the laws of life and the universe.

Ahura Mazda with Symbols of Air (Wings) and Sun (Central Wings)

The Creation of the Universe

ACCORDING TO ANCIENT SUMERIAN TRADITIONS

The Zend Avesta of Zarathustra is the first encyclopedia of mankind, dating from much farther back in recorded history than ancient Egypt, China or India. It is itself a recapitulation of previous ancient traditions, lost in the mist of history. Those early heliolithic teachings were written only in pictographs—physiograms and ideograms, which often represent a more intensive reality than abstract words formed from alphabets. To explain the Creation of the Universe in a way that would be immediately and instinctively understood, Zarathustra used these pictographs to explain the unexplainable.* "ASHA" means "the Cosmic Order," which was established through the Creation of the Universe in all its component parts. The ancient Sumerians, followers of Zarathustra, greeted each other with the words "Ashem Vohu," meaning "the Cosmic Order is the best of all things." With this greeting they stated their belief that we do not live in a capricious universe—that everything is in balance, in harmony, and to the extent that we cooperate with and strengthen this balance and harmony, we form an intrinsic part of ASHA, the Cosmic Order.

According to the Sumerian concept, everything started from a point. They chose this symbol to represent the infinity of the Creator because a point has no width, no length, no thickness, yet it contains within itself, as within each atom, an infinitesimal number of points, universes within themselves, just as our entire known universe is an infinitesimal part of innumerable unknown universes. According to their concept, at a time so remote it is impossible to imagine, there was a cosmic explosion of a point—

*Recommended reading: *Archeosophy, a New Science* and *The Zend Avesta of Zarathustra*, both by Edmond Bordeaux Szekely.

18

and this point created Time, Force, Space, and Matter. These are the pictographs used by Zarathustra to tell the story of this tremendous explosion which created our Cosmos.

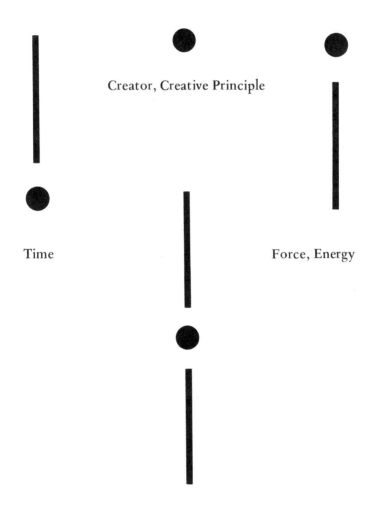

Creator, Creative Principle

Time

Force, Energy

Time and Force: Measurement of Force or Speed,
Movement of Energy in Time

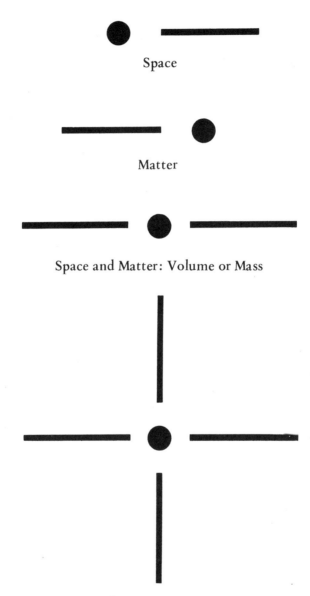

Space

Matter

Space and Matter: Volume or Mass

Creating of the Universe: Time, Space,
Force and Matter before Creation of their Modalities

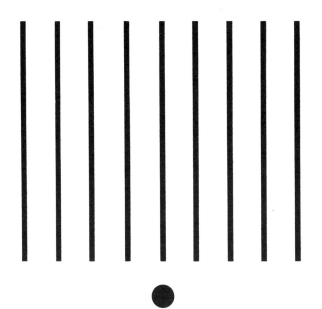

Eight Seasons: Spring, Spring-Summer, Summer,
Summer-Fall, Fall, Fall-Winter, Winter, Winter-Spring

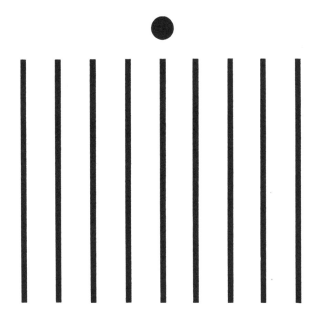

Good and Evil Energies from Stars, Sun and Earth
and those inherent in Man

Eight Cardinal Points: East, South-East, South,
South-West, West, North-West, North, North-East

Good and Evil Forms of the Four Elements:
Air, Water, Earth, Fire

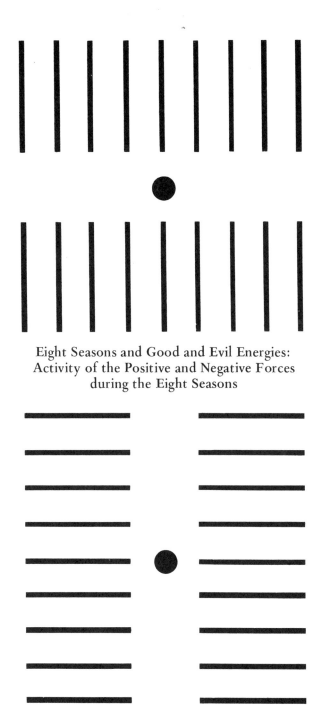

Eight Seasons and Good and Evil Energies:
Activity of the Positive and Negative Forces
during the Eight Seasons

Eight Cardinal Points Combined with
the Eight Positive and Negative Elements of Matter

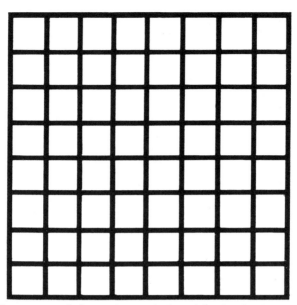

The Unity of the Universe in its Eight Basic Aspects
of Time and Space, Force and Matter,
Seasons and Cardinal Points, and their dualities

Final Cosmogonic Pictograph: Division of the Universe
into Light and Darkness, Good and Evil

The first act of the Creator was to create Time, symbolized by a straight perpendicular line moving upward from the point. The next act of the Creator was the perpendicular line moving downward from the point, representing Force, or Energy. The two lines, one above the point and one below it, represent Time and Force together, the movement of energy in time, or the measurement of force or speed.

In the next act of creation, the point moves to the right in a horizontal line, and this signified Space. The Creator next moved in a straight line to the left from the point, symbolizing Matter. The two horizontal lines representing Space and Matter produced Volume, or Mass.

When the four lines above, below, to the left and to the right of the point were combined into a pictograph, it signified the creating of the universe; in other words, Time, Space, Force and Matter before the appearance of all their modalities. We may say it represents the cosmic nebulae, before the appearance of the solar systems and planets.

When the perpendicular line above the point, symbolizing Time, was multiplied by eight, four lines to the right of the perpendicular line, and four lines to the left of it, these lines represented Time divided into the eight seasons of the year, classified by Zarathustra as spring, spring-summer, summer, summer-fall, fall, fall-winter, winter, winter-spring.

The line symbolizing Force, moving downward from the central point, was also multiplied by eight. The division of Force into eight categories introduced a new idea into their cosmogony. They first divided Force into four categories: the energies coming from the stars, those from the sun, those from the earth, and those inherent in man. But each of these four was divided once again, into good and evil, or to be more correct, light and darkness. Here appears the first idea of duality, the first dualistic philosophy in the history of human thought, represented by those eight perpendicular lines below the creating point.

When the horizontal line to the right of the point was multiplied by eight, it represented Space divided into the eight cardinal points: east, south-east, south, south-west, west, north-west, north, and north-east.

The horizontal line to the left of the point, symbolizing Matter, became the four elements: air, water, earth and fire, when multiplied by four. These four were then divided into eight, each signifying the good or evil form of the element.

The next movment of the Creator combined the two groups of perpendicular lines, those above and those below the point. Thus the symbols of the eight seasons, combined with the symbols of the eight forces, represented the activity of the positive and negative forces during the eight seasons.

The eight horizontal lines to the left of the point and the eight to the right of it were then made into a pictograph signifying the combination of the eight cardinal points of Space with eight positive and negative elements of Matter. And the final step was to divide these sixty-four squares into good and evil, light and darkness.

This pattern of thirty-two white squares and thirty-two black squares represented to the ancient Sumerians the unity of the universe as it existed around them, in its eight basic aspects of time and space, force and matter, seasons and cardinal points, and their dualities. There could be no simpler way to explain the Creation, yet in its geometric clarity is hidden all the mysteries of the Universe.

According to the ancient Sumerians, there are two aspects—light and darkness—to everything which exists. For instance, light manifests in our bodies as health, and darkness as disease. Light manifests in our minds as harmonious thoughts, darkness as disharmonious thoughts. Light manifests in nature as animals useful to man, such as the cow and the horse; while darkness manifests in creatures harmful to man, such as snakes or jaguars. Everything has two aspects in life, in our bodies, our minds, in human society, on our planet, in the universe, everywhere—there is a constant battle raging between the forces of Light and the forces of Darkness. At first, this seems a classic dualistic concept, but in its quintessence, it is more complex. For darkness is only the absence of light, and disease is only the absence of health. Disharmonious thoughts and emotions are only the absence of harmonious thoughts and emotions, and so on. Therefore, this philosophy not only represents dualism, but also monism. And this most ancient of all philosophies found its most profound expression in the exquisite language of the Art of Asha.

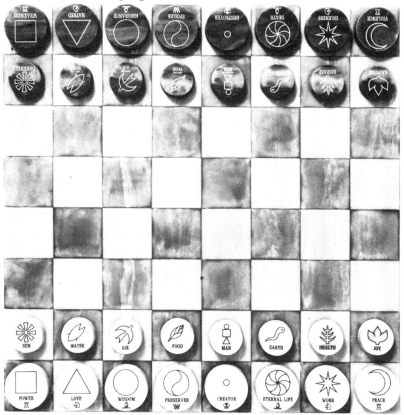

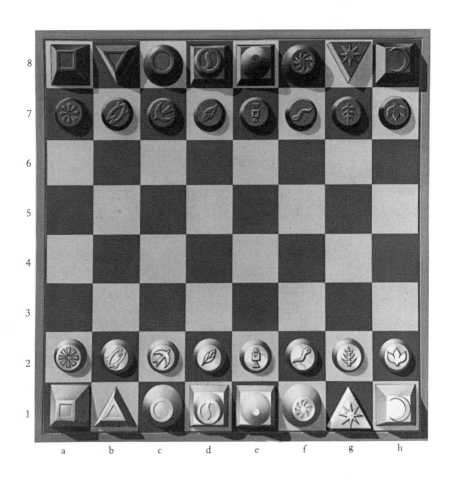

Ancient Symbols of the Natural and Cosmic Forces
in their Aspects of Light and Darkness
Gathered for the Enactment of ASHA
on the Sumerian Tapestry of Creation
(with algebraic notation)

The Creation of the World

ACCORDING TO THE ZEND AVESTA

After the Creation of the Universe, we have sixty-four squares divided between Light and Darkness, representing the Cosmos. These sixty-four squares are a kind of stage upon which the drama of Creation is enacted, as life on our planet is created. In the Zend Avesta, this event is told in the form of a dialogue between Ahura Mazda, the Creator, and Zarathustra. Through archeological reconstruction, we can present here this dialogue of creation, watching each of the sixteen forces of nature and the cosmos bring to life the Cosmic Order, ASHA, on the great stage of the universe.

Voice of Ahura Mazda:
I, Ahura Mazda, the CREATOR:
First I have made the Kingdom of Light.
> *Voice of Zarathustra:*
> You shall use your creative powers;
> Your role on this planet
> Is to continue the work of the CREATOR!
The second of the Good Kingdoms
Which I, Ahura Mazda, created,
Was Ahura PRESERVER.
> You shall PRESERVE all useful things
> In the Kingdom of Ahura Mazda.
> You shall prevent damage
> To whatever has value; whether a tree,
> Plant, house, love, or harmony in any form!
The third of the Good Kingdoms
Which I, Ahura Mazda, created,
Was the Ahura of ETERNAL LIFE.
> To reach ETERNAL LIFE

You shall have sincerity in all you do
And with everyone you meet!
The fourth of the Good Kingdoms
Which I, Ahura Mazda, created,
Was the Ahura of WISDOM.
Gain WISDOM
Through the Good Thoughts
Of Ahura Mazda!
The fifth of the Good Kingdoms
Which I, Ahura Mazda, created,
Was the Ahura of WORK.
You shall perform your daily WORK
With honesty and efficiency!
The sixth of the Good Kingdoms
Which I, Ahura Mazda, created,
Was the Ahura of LOVE.
You shall speak
Only gentle and kind words
Through the LOVE of Ahura Mazda!
The seventh of the Good Kingdoms
Which I, Ahura Mazda, created,
Was the Ahura of PEACE.
You shall maintain PEACE,
Create it within yourself and around you.
Prevent inharmony, enmity and violence!
The eighth of the Good Kingdoms
Which I, Ahura Mazda, created,
Was the Ahura of POWER.
You shall perform good deeds
Through the POWER of Ahura Mazda!
The ninth of the Good Kingdoms
Which I, Ahura Mazda, created,
Was the Fravashi of SUN.
You shall expose your body

To the Golden Rays of the SUN!
The tenth of the Good Kingdoms
Which I, Ahura Mazda, created,
Was the Fravashi of WATER.
You shall purify yourself with water
Every morning, and drink every day
The Life-giving WATER of Ahura Mazda!
The eleventh of the Good Kingdoms
Which I, Ahura Mazda, created,
Was the Fravashi of AIR.
You shall be outdoors
And breathe the Life-giving AIR
Of Ahura Mazda!
The twelfth of the Good Kingdoms
Which I, Ahura Mazda, created,
Was the Fravashi of EARTH.
You shall create more abundant life
On this EARTH by growing plants
And begetting children!
The thirteenth of the Good Kingdoms
Which I, Ahura Mazda, created,
Was the Fravashi of FOOD.
You shall eat living FOOD
From the gardens of Ahura Mazda!
The fourteenth of the Good Kingdoms
Which I, Ahura Mazda, created,
Was the Fravashi of HEALTH.
You shall use all good forces:
Sun, Water, Air, Food, Man, Earth and Joy.
Harmony with all good forces
Will give you vibrant HEALTH!
The fifteenth of the Good Kingdoms
Which I, Ahura Mazda, created,
Was the Fravashi of MAN.

> Oh, MAN! You shall strive incessantly
> On the ascending path toward the
> Light of Ahura Mazda!

The sixteenth of the Good Kingdoms
Which I, Ahura Mazda, created,
Was the Fravashi of JOY.

> Be always JOYOUS and happy
> In the Service of the Law!

An Ancient Representation of the Art of Asha

Sun *(right top)* as Cosmic Fire
Fire on Altar *(right bottom)* as Planetary Fire
Zarathustra or Mazdean Priest *(left bottom)* as Internal Fire of Life
Ahura Mazda, the Creator *(center top)* as Cosmic Ocean of Thought

The Whole represents Communion between Man and the Cosmos

As we will see in greater detail later, when we learn the rules of the Art of Asha, each of these sixteen natural and cosmic forces represents one source of energy, harmony and knowledge at our disposal, for us to use in our lives— one force in the field of forces surrounding man. The positive forces of nature were called Fravashis, and the positive forces of the cosmos were called Ahuras. Together they formed the Army of Light of Ahura Mazda, the Creator. Their opposites on the side of Darkness were the Khrafstras and the Devas, led by the Destroyer, Ahriman. But as the negative forces represent only the absence of Light, they are not included in this re-enactment of the Creation of Life on our planet, this powerful dialogue between Ahura Mazda and Zarathustra, between the Creator and Man, whose role it is to continue the work of creation on earth.

On the tapestry of ASHA, Man, one of the sixteen forces, stands directly in front of the Creator. This means that we have a duty and a right at the same time: a duty to establish harmony with all these sixteen forces, and the privilege to absorb these forces as sources of harmony, energy and knowledge. According to the Zend Avesta, we live in a dynamic universe, and we must know how to respond to these forces which permanently surround us and flow toward us. Intelligence is the ability to adapt ourselves adequately to unexpected changes in our environment, and this parallelogram of forces which surrounds us is constantly changing. Therefore, we must learn to adapt our thoughts, our words and our deeds to each one of these forces, so we can learn to utilize their energy, harmony and knowledge.

The Art of Asha is a universe within itself, a collection of various methods employing music, drama, art, weaving, gardening, even self-analysis, in order to keep our attention fixed on the reality of these forces in every segment of our daily lives. For these forces are realities, not sterile metaphysical speculation, or dry scriptural abstractions. Every one of the sixteen forces is a tangible part of the world we live in, from the air we breathe and the food we eat, to the joy we feel and the wisdom we seek. "Good thoughts, good words, good deeds. . ." these words of Zarathustra are the most simple and direct of all moral codes. We will learn through the Art of Asha how to use them to further our own individual evolution, as well as that of our planet.

Ancient representation
of two Mazdean Priests and Tree of Life
with symbol of Ahura Mazda (Wings and Sun) above

THE COSMIC ORDER with SUMERIAN SYMBOLS
QUOTATIONS FROM THE ZEND AVESTA
& MUSICAL INTERPRETATIONS

SUN

Up! Rise up and roll along!
Thou immortal, shining,
Swift-steeded Sun!
Above the Mountains!
Produce Light for the World!

WATER

From the Cosmic Sea the Waters run and flow forward
From the never-failing Springs . . .

AIR

We worship the Holy Breath
Which is placed higher
Than all the other things created . . .

FOOD

Golden-hued plants grow up from the Earth during the Spring
And impart their gifts of Food unto Men.

MAN

The Teacher of the Law will stride forth
Upon this Earth among its dwellers!
It is for the choice of man by man,
Each individually for himself,
To recognize the great impulse of the cause of ASHA.
Then will he labor to complete the progress
And renovation of the World.

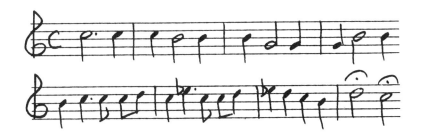

EARTH

This wide Earth do I praise,
Expanded far with paths,
The productive, the full-bearing,
Thy Mother, Holy Plant!

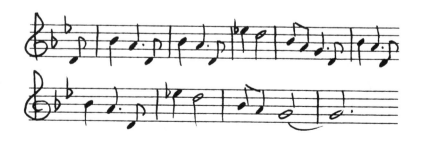

HEALTH

. . . for the vigor of Health, Health of the Body,
Wise, bright and clear-eyed, with swiftness of foot,
Quick hearing of the ears, strength of the arms
And eye-sight of the eagle . . .

JOY

ASHA is the Best of All Good.

It is also Happiness.

Happy is the man who is Holy through ASHA.

POWER

Thine, O Ahura Mazda!
Was the Power, when Thou didst order
A Path for each of us and all.
And this Teaching was the first of all rules
To regulate our actions.
He is most helpful and vigorous
Who serves with every Power,
Preserving and nurturing Thy Cosmic Order
Through the fulfillment of Deeds.

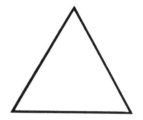

LOVE

O Gracious Love!

Demonstrate Spiritual Truth through Thy Cosmic Order.

O Creator of Love! Reveal the Best Words

Through Thy Good Mind living within us.

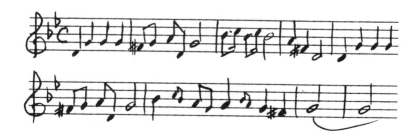

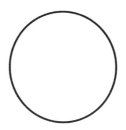

WISDOM

Holy Wisdom maketh man free from anxiety,
Wide of heart, and easy of Conscience.
Holy Wisdom, the Understanding that continuously unfolds
And is not acquired through Learning.

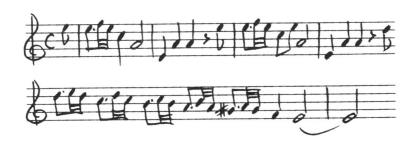

PRESERVER

The Holy Preserver! The Maintainer!
It is She Who will restore the World!
Which will thenceforth never grow old and never die!
Ever living and ever increasing . ...
When Creation will grow deathless . . .

◯

CREATOR

First, O Great Creator!

Thou didst create the Cosmic Powers

And Thou didst reveal the Cosmic Laws!

Thou gavest unto us understanding from Thine Own Mind!

And Thou madst our bodily life.

Thou didst determine all our actions by Thy Power.

SILENCE

ETERNAL LIFE

We follow the paths of the Stars,
The Moon, the Sun and the endless Light,
Moving around in their revolving circle Forever.
And Truthfulness in Thought, Word and Deed
Will place the Soul of faithful man
In the endless light of Eternal Life.

WORK

My name is the Worker of Good,

Because I work the good of the Creator.

My name is the spirit, conscience and soul of the Great men

Who teach the Law and who struggle for ASHA.

PEACE

I will invoke Peace, whose breath is friendly,
Who is more powerful than all other creatures.
In the reign of Peace, there is neither hunger nor thirst,
Neither cold wind nor hot wind,
Neither old age nor death.

We are no other than a moving row
Of Magic Shadow-shapes that come and go
  Round with the Sun-illumined Lantern held
In Midnight by the Master of the Show;

We fearlessly defend Him as He plays
Upon this Chequer-board of Nights and Days;
  Hither and thither moves, and checks, and wins,
And then another Universe begins.

Ormuzd in wondrous Strength and Brilliance grows,
Whilst Ahriman in deeps of darkness goes,
  And He Who guided all with His own hand,
He knows about it all—He knows—He knows!

        from the 11th century Persian poet
                Omar Khayyam

THE ANCIENT PERSIAN LEGEND AND

The Art of Asha

Through a beautiful Persian legend, the ancient Art of Asha
is linked with what we know as chess today, referred to
throughout history as "the game of kings and the king of
games." But while today's chess is only a game, the ancient
Art of Asha is *not* a game; it is a profoundly complex and
intricately-woven microcosm within the macrocosm of
Life— a complete universe within itself.

The word chess derives from the Persian "Shah," meaning
King, which originally was "Asha," the Cosmic Order.
The legend survives that King Vishtaspa of Persia became
extremely bored with life, for he had accomplished everything he wished: he was satiated with triumphs in war,
tired of hunting, surfeited with the intrigues and pleasures
of his court. The King suffered from ennui and finally
offered an unlimited reward to the man who could give him
some interest in life. No one was successful until Zarathustra
appeared with the original, undistorted form of today's
chess: the Art of Asha. He taught the King the rules and
how to enact it, and through it demonstrated to the King all
the laws of the universe and life. He interpreted them as
he alone could do, as no present day chess player would
think to do, and the King was extremely satisfied and his
interest in life was renewed. He thereupon told Zarathustra
to ask for whatever he might want and said it should be
given him. Zarathustra wished to give the King a lesson which
would teach him not to be so megalomanic as to think he
could give anyone everything he wanted. So Zarathustra
told the king he wanted only a very simple and modest
thing: one grain of wheat on the first square of the chess
board, two on the second square, the square of two on the

third square, the square of that on the fourth square, and so on until all sixty-four squares were filled with the square of the amount on the previous square. The King laughed and said he would send Zarathustra the wheat in a few days, thinking what a fool he was to ask only for a few grains of wheat when he could have had gold and fine treasure. He told his men to calculate the amount of wheat and send it to Zarathustra. He was surprised when, after several weeks, they came to him and told him the quantity of wheat which he should deliver to Zarathustra was more than that in the whole kingdom. Even if he gathered together all the wheat in the empire, it would not be one-thousandth of one-thousandth of the amount he had promised to Zarathustra. The King was very shocked to learn this and to know that he could not fulfill his promise. He sent for Zarathustra and told him how ashamed he was. Zarathustra answered that he did not want the wheat; he only wanted to teach the King a lesson, and he thereupon retired to his forest. This is the ancient legend about the origin of chess—the Art of Asha—which traces chess back to ancient Persia. Unfortunately, chess today is only a pastime, a faint echo of the original Art of Asha, although it partially observes the ancient Sumerian symbology.

Though archeological proofs of the origin of chess may be lacking, there is no doubt that chess had its beginning in the east many thousands of years ago. The original chess was the Art of Asha, and its function was to symbolize and exemplify the natural and cosmic laws represented by the Ahuras (cosmic forces), the Fravashis (natural forces), and their shadows. In the Art of Asha is found a microcosmos: each enactment represents in miniature the eternal cosmic battle between good and evil, light and darkness.

The Art of Asha represents a vital bridge of understanding between the universal, all-encompassing world-conception of Zarathustra and his practical, daily application of the Ashaic system of self-analysis. To enact the Art of Asha is to bring into focus the vast universal conception of Zarathustra and to apply its rules to daily life. The more one takes part in the Art of Asha, the more one comprehends the unique role of Man, the center figure on the chessboard, the most important of the Fravashis, partner of the Creator and the one who must carry on the work of Creation on earth.

As the rules of ASHA are learned, it is fascinating to observe how the movements of the various figures assume a far more vast and universal meaning as we replace the modern chess names with the ancient, original ones. For example, Power and Peace, at each end in the first rank, move vertically and horizontally, indicating sweeping motions of infinite strength. They are second in importance only to the Preserver in assuring the triumph of Light over Darkness. Love and Work, like the Knight in chess, move in ingenious patterns, and are the only figures which may jump over any other figure. Thus, obstacles which may exist for other forces do not exist for them, recalling to mind the words of the Bible, "Love is stronger than death," and the ancient Roman proverb, "Work overcomes all evil." The Creator is able to move only one square at a time in any direction, while the Preserver has great versatility and may move any distance in any direction. This symbolizes that while the creation of the universe may have taken place in a moment of time, the rest of eternity is given to the Preserver to make eternal that which has been created. What the King's Pawn is to modern chess, in the Art of Asha, is Man. The words of Protagoras come to mind: "Man is the measure of all things." Man occupies the most glorious place on the board: directly in front of the Creator, symbolizing his eternal unity with the Law of Laws and his unique role of representative of the Creator on earth.

". . . I am Life fighting nothingness. I am the Fire which burns in the Night. I am the Eternal Light. I am free Will which struggles eternally. Struggle and burn with me. . . though thou art conquered, yet art thou of the army which is never vanquished. For ages death has hunted Me and nothingness has lain in wait for Me. It is only by victory in the fight that I can make My way. Darkness hems Me in and I hurl it down. *And the rhythm of the battle is the Supreme Harmony. . .*"

—Romain Rolland, Jean Christophe.

THE ART OF THE COSMIC ORDER AND THE

Rules of the Art of Asha

The board on which the Art of Asha is enacted represents the universe, woven out of Time, Space, Force and Matter *(see p. 20)*. According to ancient Sumerian tradition, the Creator created the universe by sixteen successive movements until it was divided into Light and Darkness *(see p. 24)*.

The symbols, of which there are sixteen on either side, stand for the natural and cosmic forces—both positive and negative—which operate within the framework of the universe. They symbolize the Zarathustrian cosmology, just as the board represents its cosmogony.

The purpose of the Art of Asha is to teach and illustrate the perpetual struggle going on between the positive and negative forces in the universe, a battle of opposing forces which gives birth to life. The positive forces of Light are represented by Ahura Mazda and his army, and the negative forces of darkness by Ahriman and his army.

THE BOARD AND ITS SYMBOLS

ASHA is played on a board of sixty-four squares, alternately light and dark in color, which are commonly referred to as "white" or "black." The horizontal rows of squares are called "ranks" and the vertical rows "files." The board is set between the players so that there is a white square at the right end of the first rank next to each player.

Each of the two players has sixteen symbols at his command. Ahura Mazda, the Creator, has with him in his army seven other Ahuras or creative cosmic forces—making eight in all—and eight Fravashis or forces of nature. These are the symbols of the positive forces in the Zarathustrian system of cosmology.

In the opposing army of Ahriman are the shadows of each of the positive symbols in Ahura Mazda's army. These are the unfriendly and destructive cosmic forces—the "black" symbols on the board. Eight of them are called Devas and are the shadows of the Ahuras, while eight are called Khrafstras and are the shadows of the Fravashis. These thirty-two symbols are set on the board as shown in the illustration, with the Ahuras and Devas in the first rank on either side of the board. The Fravashis and Khrafstras, the lesser forces of each army, are set in the second rank—from the viewpoint of each of the players.

The symbols for the positive and negative forces are the same in form and outline, but those of Ahura Mazda are white, while their shadows, the army of Ahriman, are black. However, each black symbol has its own name and is not known by the name of its white counterpart in the army of Ahura Mazda. Thus the shadow of the Creator is called the Destroyer, the shadow of the Preserver is the Spoiler, etc.

The symbols of the Ahuras, the invisible creative forces in the army of Ahura Mazda, occupy the first rank on their side of the board. They consist of, first, the Creator and the Preserver, which occupy the two center squares on the first rank of the "white" end of the board; the Preserver always occupies a square of its own color, as does its shadow, the Spoiler. The Creator and the Preserver (and their opposites) are distinguished from each other by the moves they may make during the play.

Flanking the Preserver is Wisdom and flanking the Creator is Eternal Life. Wisdom and Eternal Life move in the same manner and are of equal rank. Respectively flanking them are Love and Work, another pair of equal rank and subject to the same rules. Power and Peace occupy the left and right corner squares: they move in accordance with the same rules and restrictions.

The Fravashis, the visible forces of nature, are set on the second rank of Ahura Mazda's side of the board. From left to right, they are as follows: Sun, Water, Air, Food, Man, Earth, Health, and Joy. These symbols form a group, all members of which move under the same rules and are subject to the same restrictions.

The Devas and Khrafstras—the shadows of the sixteen positive symbols—are placed in like manner at the opposite end of the board, occupying the same files as their counterparts. Each shadow is of equal rank with its counterpart and follows the same rules and is subject to the same restrictions.

While the object of chess, the distant descendant of the Art of Asha, is to overcome and capture the opposing king, so that he has no hope of escape (called "checkmate"), the object of ASHA is quite different. While one side or the other may well arrive at "checkmate," it is the drama of Life itself, the endlessly fascinating and eternally evolving battle of opposing forces that is the real "object." The microcosmos of ASHA teaches the players how to cooperate with the positive forces of Light in order to overcome the negative forces of darkness, and it is in the learning of these important lessons that the real object of ASHA is realized, regardless of which "side" a player may be on at the time.

HOW THE SYMBOLS MOVE

The two players "move" one of their symbols alternately. In one case only, to be explained later, may they move two symbols at the same time. A move consists of changing the position of a symbol by moving it from one square to another. The player fighting Ahura Mazda's battle always has the first move. Passing up a move is not permitted.

Symbols may only be moved over unoccupied squares and must come to rest either in an unoccupied square or in one occupied by a symbol of the opposing army. Exceptions to this are the symbols of Love, Work and their shadows, Hatred and Idleness, which can leap over their opponents in the manner described later.

A player who has touched one of his opponent's symbols with the intention of taking it must take it if it can legally be taken. If he touches one in order to adjust it, he must say "I adjust." When a player takes his hand off a symbol he has moved, then the move is complete and he cannot put the symbol back where it came from.

One symbol captures (x) another by being moved into the square occupied by the latter. The captured symbol is removed from the board and the capturing symbol occupies its square. Capturing is optional unless the Creator or Destroyer is threatened, in which case it is compulsory.

MOVES OF THE AHURAS AND DEVAS

The Creator and his shadow, the Destroyer, move in accordance with rules applicable to them alone.

Similarly, the Preserver and her shadow, the Spoiler, move under rules peculiar to them alone, enjoying more freedom than any of the other symbols on the board.

The remaining six Ahuras and their six shadows fall into patterns of four, each pattern consisting of two Ahuras and the two corresponding Devas. The two Ahuras of a pattern are always in the same position relative to the left and right edges of the board, while their shadows are always in the same file at the opposite end of the board. The symbols forming a pattern also operate under the same rules and are subject to the same restrictions.

Thus, Power and Peace move in accordance with the same rules and occupy the left and right corner squares of the first rank, and their shadows move in the same way and occupy the corner squares at their end of the board. Love and Work, moving under a different rule, stand just inside

Power and Peace. Wisdom and Eternal Life, governed by still different rules of movement, take the squares third from the outer edge of the board.

The symbols are grouped into patterns (determining their position in relation to each other and their rules of movement) as follows:

AHURA—FORCE	DEVA—SHADOW
Power	Weakness
Peace	Violence
Love	Hatred
Work	Idleness
Wisdom	Ignorance
Eternal Life	Death

MOVES OF POWER AND PEACE AND THEIR SHADOWS

Power, Peace, Weakness and Violence can move either horizontally or vertically, forward or backward, in one direction at a time, along any rank or file in which they happen to stand at the time of the move, provided that no other symbol of their own army obstructs the path. If an opposing symbol stands on the square to which any of these four symbols move, it is captured and removed from the board. These four symbols command fourteen squares if the path is unobstructed in all directions.

MOVES OF LOVE AND WORK AND THEIR SHADOWS

The moves of Love, Work and their shadows, Hatred and Idleness, offer some difficulty, as they are not confined to rank, file or diagonal like the other players. However, their moves are not hard to grasp if they are thought of as a jump or leap to the next square but one of the opposite color. The leap is made by moving one square in a rank and then two squares in a file, or one square in a file and two squares in a rank. In this move one symbol can jump over another symbol of its own or the hostile army. If the leap is from a white square, it will be to a black square, and vice versa.

As in the case of the other plays, the symbol making this move can only capture an opposing symbol if it is located on a square on which the moving symbol comes to rest: a symbol on the square over which the moving symbol jumps is not captured.

MOVES OF WISDOM, ETERNAL LIFE AND THEIR SHADOWS

The symbols of Wisdom, Eternal Life, Ignorance and Death move backward and forward to any square on the diagonals on which they happen to stand, provided the path is not obstructed by a symbol of the same color as their own. They capture a hostile symbol in their path by occupying the square on which it stands. They are confined to squares of the same color as the ones on which they originally stood. They are thus able to reach only thirty-two squares on the board and are therefore less powerful than Power, Peace and their shadows which have access to all sixty-four squares.

MOVES OF THE PRESERVER AND ITS SHADOW, THE SPOILER

These are the two most powerful symbols. They can move forward, backward, sidewise or diagonally, in any direction and to any square on the rank, file or diagonal on which they stand, provided their path is not obstructed by another symbol of their own army. They capture a hostile symbol in their path by occupying the square on which it stands.

MOVES OF THE CREATOR AND ITS SHADOW, THE DESTROYER

The Creator and Destroyer may move and capture in any direction and to squares of either color, but can move only one square at a time and only to squares on which they cannot be captured by a hostile symbol.

These two symbols differ from all the others in that they cannot be captured and removed from the board.

If a hostile symbol moves in such a way that on its next

move the Creator (or Destroyer) could be captured by it, it is said to "attack" the Creator and the Creator is then in "check."

The player whose Creator (or Destroyer) is in check must get it out of check or the attack will become a "checkmate" and this particular scene in the eternal battle of opposing forces will come to an end.

The Creator and Destroyer can never occupy adjoining squares on the board, but must always have at least one square between them, as neither can "check" the other.

MOVES OF THE FRAVASHIS AND KHRAFSTRAS

Fravashis: *Sun, Water, Air, Food, Man, Earth, Health, Joy.*

Khrafstras: *Darkness, Impure Water, Impure Air, Impure Food, Inferior Man, Barrenness, Disease, Sadness.*

The symbols of the eight Fravashis and eight Khrafstras all follow the same particular rules. They are the only symbols to move in one direction and capture in another. They move *only forward,* straight ahead in the file in which they stand—except that on their first move they may advance two squares.

They capture only forward *diagonally,* moving only one square at a time. They never move or capture backward or sideways. Any symbol placed directly in front of a Fravashi or Khrafstra stops its further advance, as it can only move forward yet cannot capture the symbol blocking its forward move.

If one of these symbols reaches the eighth rank, it is "promoted" in the manner described later.

RESTING

Once in each enactment of ASHA the player fighting Ahura Mazda's battle may move two symbols at the same time: either the Creator and Power, or the Creator and Peace. This procedure is called "resting" and consists of a double step of the Creator toward the other symbol used in the move and the placing of that other symbol on the square over which the Creator has passed. The shadow of the Creator, the Destroyer, has the same privilege.

Resting is only permitted if neither the Creator nor the other symbol involved in the battle has moved previously, if the path between the two is unobstructed, and if none of the three squares affected by the Creator's move is within range of a hostile symbol. Resting is restricted to the three symbols of Ahura Mazda mentioned above and to their shadows.

Neither the Creator nor the Destroyer can "rest" to get out of check, or through a position which is in check, or "rest" into check, or "rest" into a square occupied by a hostile symbol. However, the other symbol taking part in the resting move, e.g. Power, is not affected by check.

CAPTURING "IN PASSING"

If a Fravashi which would be captured by a Khrafstra (or vice versa) if it advanced one square, seeks to avoid capture by exercising its privilege of making a double step forward, then the opposing player may put it back one square and capture it. This procedure, called capturing "in passing," is available only to Fravashis and their shadows.

The symbol making the capture must be standing on the fifth rank and the symbol it captures must be making its first move. The move by which the symbol makes the capture must be the move immediately after the double step of the opposing symbol in the play.

PROMOTING

The Fravashis and their shadows, the Khrafstras, are also subject to a procedure which may appropriately be termed "promoting," as by it they are promoted to a higher status.

Whenever a Fravashi or a Khrafstra reaches the eighth rank without being captured, its player has to exchange it for a symbol of higher rank and of its own color, i.e., an

Ahura or a Deva, as the case may be, using for this purpose a duplicate symbol. Any symbol may be chosen with the exception of the Creator or Destroyer.

It can thus happen that the player fighting Ahura Mazda's battle may have more than one Preserver, or more than one Love or Wisdom on the board, while Ahriman's side may have more than one Spoiler or Idleness. As the Preserver and Spoiler are the strongest symbols available for the exchange, they are almost always chosen.

CHECK AND CHECKMATE

There is one exception to the rule that the player may make the move of his choosing. This is when the Creator or Destroyer is attacked in such a way that it could be captured on the next move of a hostile symbol. It is then said to be in "check" (†) and it is then the duty of the player whose symbol is checked to get it out of check before making any other move.

Unless the attacking symbol can be captured, the symbol in check can only be protected by moving it to a square on which it is not liable to attack or by interposing a symbol between the symbol in check and the one attacking.

As already mentioned, the Creator or Destroyer must be got out of check or its player forfeits that particular scene of the battle. If unable to get out, it is said to be "checkmate." (††)

KEEPING A RECORD

A method of recording the moves is needed, and for this purpose an algebraic system of notation is used which serves to identify every square on the board. In this system the files are lettered from A to H, proceeding from left to right from Ahura Mazda's end of the board. The ranks are numbered 1 to 8, counting from below upward from Ahura Mazda's viewpoint. By combining number and letter any square on the board can be easily identified.

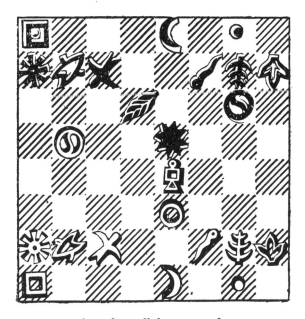

Examples of Parallelograms of Forces
in Different Phases of the Cosmic Battle
between the Armies of Ahura Mazda and Ahriman

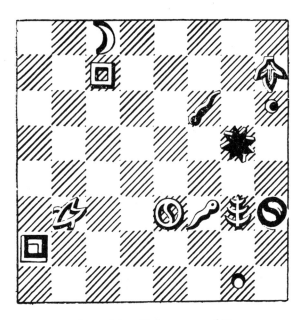

Examples of Parallelograms of Forces
in Different Phases of the Cosmic Battle
between the Armies of Ahura Mazda and Ahriman

THE COSMIC DRAMA OF THE ROYAL BATTLE

from a tenth century poem by Firdusi
author of the National Epic of Persia, the "Shah Nama"
adapted by him from the sixth century Pahlavian "Khwatai-Namak"

In the beginning of the reign, the armies stand before thee. Thine eyes shall see the Creator in His glory.

Behold, He standeth at the head of all His hosts; He shall cry, yea, He shall shout aloud; He shall do mightily against His enemies. By the strength of His hand He shall bring down to the dust the Destroyer and all those who follow him.

The Preserver doth stand at His left hand; the Creator looketh upon her with favor.

Nigh unto them are the triangle of Love and the star of Work; at their left and at their right the circle of Wisdom and the wheel of Eternal Life; and at each end the square of Power and the crescent moon of Peace.

These are the sacred Cosmic forces and their ways are of mystery; their secrets unfolded only to those who give their lives in order to Know.

Guarding the Holy symbols are the forces of Nature; though each may venture forth only timidly at the outset of battle, their power is not lightly to be judged, for in their hands is often the safety and welfare of the Cosmic forces, and though their feet are straight feet, if it be their will to capture the followers of the Destroyer, they may diverge to either flank. And should one of their number reach the forbidden camp of the Destroyer, the haven of his desire, lo! he skippeth as a hart! Then he is swifter than the eagles of heaven, he hasteneth his steps, and doeth that in which his soul delighteth, even all that the Preserver doeth.

Behold the names of these Eight Warriors of Nature and remember them well: the rays of the Sun; the fish of

Water; the bird of Air; the wheat-grain of Food; the figure of Man; the earthworm of Earth; the tree of Health; and the flower of Joy.

Now let thy range of vision be all-encompassing as I display before thee the marchings and counter-marchings of this army, and I will explain in lucid words the marvelous movements of these timeless warriors.

When the Creator marcheth from place to place in His dominion, there is but one Law for Him, whether His course be flank-wise or straight; all that He desireth He doeth; but His heart is not ambitious to extend His range in battle, lest He should die in the war. From His shielded fortress He guides the steps of His brave warriors, for to Him they look ever for inspiration and fresh valor.

The wheel of Eternal Life and the circle of Wisdom advance without divergence in oblique direction, bent in their path on victory, and they turn not aside. Behold them rushing forth, and whither they go, they work utter desolation to the army of the Destroyer.

And the triangle of Love and the star of Work set themselves in array at the gate. For these there are no obstacles; it is given them that they may fly with wings over the enemy. In glory they go forth, forward one pace, then oblique, in a sacred dance of victory over death.

Before the square of Power and the crescent moon of Peace lies a straight path, their movements being the same on their four sides. They turn not when they go. They march along the whole length of the path which is before them. Alone, each is formidable; together, they are invincible. For when Power is tempered with Peace, it is incorruptible; and when Peace has as its bulwark Power, it is imperishable.

Behold, I have laid before thee goodly words, to teach thee to obey the commands of the Creator and his decree, whithersoever they may reach thee. I have shown thee the laws of the contest, its genius, and its principles, and there lacketh not one about whom I have not written.

Excepting that we have not yet spoken of the Preserver. She sitteth at the top of the high places of the city. She is clamorous and wilful in her way. She girdeth her loins with strength. Her feet abide not in her house. She moveth in all directions, and turneth about her. Her evolutions are wonderful, her ardor untiring. How beautiful are her steps across the plain!

And the Destroyer, clad in black garments, draweth nigh unto the thick darkness where standeth the Spoiler. Together they shall come out against the Holy Army with one movement and one journey. If they be not cautious, as the one dieth, so dieth the other.

And now the Kings of Good and Evil intrigue against each other, and pursue each other unto the death. The Destroyer is embarrassed in the fight; and when he resteth in his place, a Warrior of the Creator may command him to go forth from his boundary, lest he should smite him with destruction. He may retreat in any direction; but if in striving to escape his feet be caught in the snare set by the warriors that surround him, then is his glory turned into destruction. And the Army of Death who are left after him are as nothing; for of what account are they? In one moment they are subdued: Darkness, Impure Water, Impure Air, Impure Food, Inferior Man, Barrenness, Disease, Sadness, Weakness, Hatred, Ignorance, the Spoiler, Death, Idleness, Violence; and their commander, the Destroyer, is brought low, he is thrust out, he boweth down, and he falleth. The Creator who hath striven against him bringeth him down from his greatness. And the Creator is left in glory and majesty, and His Holy Warriors of Nature and the Cosmos sing a joyful hymn of thanksgiving that the power of Light has overthrown the Darkness.

Thus shall perish all the enemies of the Creator, and they that seek His destruction; but they that love Him shall be as the sun when he goeth forth in his glory.

The archeological reconstruction of the ancient Zarathustrian ceremony of the Creation of the Universe is an important part of International Biogenic Society Seminars. *(above)* Dr. Edmond Bordeaux Szekely in 1967 at Mille Meditations, California. *(below)* Norma Nilsson Bordeaux Szekely in 1980 at the I.B.S. International Center in Orosi, Costa Rica.

*Outdoor life-size archeological reconstruction
of ASHA. Orosi, Costa Rica.*

"Man is not alone
On the Chessboard of Life.
He is surrounded by Divine Powers,
Love and Wisdom,
and all the good forces of Providence
in this world of Shadows and Lights."

—Tolstoy

Chess Can Be Translated Into a Cosmic Drama
IF WE APPLY THE KEY OF ASHA

When Chess is translated, through algebraic notation, into the language of the Art of Asha, it becomes a profoundly meaningful and stirring Cosmic Drama. This match was played between the great Russian novelist, Leo Tolstoy, and a German Chess champion, Fritz Kuhler.

Count Leo Tolstoy	Fritz Kuhler
1. Man E2–E4	Inferior Man E7–E5
2. Work G1–F3	Hatred B8–C6
3. Eternal Life F1–C4	Death F8–C5
4. Air C2–C3	Idleness G8–F6
5. Food D2–D4	Inferior Man E5 X Food D4
6. Air C3 X Inferior Man D4	Death C5–B4†
7. Love B1–C3	Idleness F6 X Man E4
8. Creator E1-G1 Peace H1-F1	Idleness E4 X Love C3
9. Water B2 X Idleness C3	Death B4 X Water C3
10. Preserver D1–B3	Death C3 X Power A1
11. Eternal Life C4 X Barrenness F7†	Destroyer E8–F8
12. Wisdom C1–G5	Hatred C6–E7
13. Peace F1–E1	Impure Food D7–D5
14. Eternal Life F7 X Impure Food D5	Spoiler D8–D7
15. Wisdom G5 X Hatred E7†	Spoiler D7 X Wisdom E7
16. Peace E1 X Spoiler E7	Destroyer F8 X Peace E7
17. Preserver B3–E3†	Destroyer E7–D8
18. Preserver E3–G5†	Destroyer D8–E8
19. Preserver G5 X Disease G7	Violence H8–F8
20. Work F3–G5	Sadness H7–H5
21. Work G5–H7	Violence F8–F5
22. Work H7–F6†	Violence F5 X Work F6
23. Preserver G7 X Violence F6	Death A1–B2
24. Eternal Life D5–F7†	Destroyer E8–F8
25. Eternal Life F7–G6†	Destroyer F8–G8
26. Preserver F6–F7†	Destroyer G8–H8
27. Preserver F7–H7††	

...and the Army of Ahura Mazda triumphs over the Kingdom of Ahriman!

Chess Can Be Translated Into a Symphony

IF WE APPLY THE KEY OF ASHA

Chess Can Be Translated Into a Symphony

IF WE APPLY THE KEY OF ASHA

Chess Can Be Translated Into a Symphony

IF WE APPLY THE KEY OF ASHA

Chess Can Be Translated Into a Symphony

IF WE APPLY THE KEY OF ASHA

Chess Can Be Translated Into a Symphony

IF WE APPLY THE KEY OF ASHA

IF WE APPLY THE KEY OF ASHA

From this one event in the life of Tolstoy, we have created, through the language of ASHA, a cosmic drama, a symphony, and a beautiful symbolic painting. Each time the forces of Light and Darkness meet in battle, cosmic dramas, symphonies, and works of art are created, continually furthering and enhancing our individual evolution, and the evolution of our planet.

Zarathustra's Avestic Cosmology
(translated into modern terminology)

Dynamism or Universal Kinetism: There is only movement. Things do not exist statically; they are formed, broken up, transformed. It is partial formations of universal movement which undergo transformation.

Matter and Thought: The most elementary dynamic formations are those of matter, matter being merely an aggregate of the movement of atoms, *while the highest dynamic formations are those of currents of thought.*

The Material Preconditions of Cosmic Evolution: The infinite variety of the dynamic formations of matter necessarily creates the preconditions of evolution towards the higher dynamic forms (the formation of the solar systems, of the planets, of the satellites, etc., the successive cooling of the planetary surfaces, of the atmosphere (air), of the seas (water) and of the solid layers (earth), and the progressive changes in the temperature (solar energy) necessary for the formation of organic life).

The Action of Inorganic Gravitation: The lower dynamic forms of matter are governed by gravitation (their mutual attractions and repulsions). Gravitation tends to blend together all the dynamic formations of matter and to draw them towards the center of each planet.

Currents of the Higher Cosmic Radiations: Organisms and Individual Consciousnesses: On the other hand, where the preconditions of the highest dynamic formations of matter are produced, the currents of the higher cosmic radiations (which are the results of earlier but practically identical evolutions) tend to group the lower dynamic formations (primitive organisms, the beginnings of and changes in the infinitely various forms of individual consciousness) round centers, just as on a huge scale the suns, planets and satellites are grouped round their centers.

The Action of Organic Gravitation (Vitality): The directive force of these dynamic formations (primitive organisms, (etc.) grouped round a center is *organic gravitation* (vitality) generated by the higher vital cosmic currents according as the preconditions for their formations exist.

Universal and Continual Struggle between Gravitation and Vitality: This vitality is the opposite of inorganic gravitation. While gravitation draws the inorganic groups towards the center of each planet, the vital force pushes the organic cellular groups in the opposite direction, away from the planetary centers towards increasingly remote higher and higher spheres.

Its Result is Life in Endless Evolutive Phases: In short, life since the time of the most primitive dynamic formations is simply composed of the resultants of these correlative forces, gravity and vitality, developed through endless evolutive phases.

The Victory of Gravitation is Death: Every organism whose vital force is overcome by gravitation breaks up into its inorganic elements and then becomes once more subject solely to gravitation (reign of death).

Reproduction, Continuity, Evolution and Liberation of Life: However, the vital force, with each new generation, gives rise to higher and higher manifestations of life in proportion to environmental conditions and the cosmic forces present permit of such manifestations (vegetation, animal kingdom, man). In these manifestations the effect of gravitation progressively decreases, while vital force increases more and more. The higher the material formation of life, the greater its ability to establish and produce in itself the cosmic vibrations of a higher type.

Law of the Degrees of Cosmic Superiority: The degree

of superiority of the material formations of life is directly proportional (a) to their ability to establish the cosmic vibrations of a higher type in such life, (b) to the faculty of producing such higher mental currents, and (c) to the degree of development reached by such mental currents.

Life on Our Planet and the Others: On our earth, the most developed form of life is at the moment represented by man. On planets older than ours incomparably higher forms of life succeed one another in infinite variety.

The Infinite — Eternity — Cosmic Purpose: Just as the cosmos and its life are unlimited, so is the changing variety of these dynamic formations without end. Consequently the aim of the infinite can only be infinite, since there is no objective already attained which cannot be transcended with the help of time and the presence of the necessary preconditions. The infinite ahead of us is as eternal as the infinite behind us. If a final, universal objective were possible, it must have already been reached. The aim of the universe can only be eternal life, by drawing its energies from its own resources, eternal generation, the dynamic formations, their destruction and improvement, eternal movement of generation, destruction and eternal improvement, improvement and perfection.

Individual Purpose: The eternal forces established in each organism by gravitation and under the influence of the cosmic currents of universal life acquire progressively greater knowledge of the world by creating more and more potent mental forces.

Union with the Higher Cosmic Currents: Final Triumph Over Gravitation: By the realization of an increasingly closer union with the higher cosmic currents, by more and more perfect adaptation to these currents, attained through utilization of and submission to the laws of nature and to their preconditions of milieu, they progressively refine their material organisms, undergo improvement, and *finally gain freedom from gravitation,* becoming more and more independent of the lowest dynamic formations of matter until their triumph over gravitation is complete.

Optimal Course of Eternal and Omnilateral Evolution: They thus maintain their own eternal sources of energy and fall in with the optimal course taken by eternal omnilateral evolution, passing through increasingly perfect formations.

Framework of Creation: White and Black Checkerboard
on Pottery. (Persepolis)

MEDITATIONS ON LIFE IN

The Zend Avesta

On the Mother of Life. . . EARTH. The basis of all manifestations of life on this planet is the top soil. The sustenance of the vegetable and animal kingdoms, as well as that of humanity and of all civilization, is based upon and depends upon these few inches of earth. This thin layer gives the necessary food to plants, which in turn provide food for all animals. Man, too, lives partly on foods from the vegetable kingdom and partly on such foods of animal origin as milk and eggs, which are also indirectly derived from the soil by way of the vegetable kingdom. There is something miraculous and mysterious in this life-giving property of soil, from which everything comes and to which everything returns. The "wheel of life" is that secret universal process whereby the various vital energies travel from the soil through the vegetable and animal kingdoms and thence back to the soil.

On the Water of Life. . . WATER is not less important than the soil as the bearer of life, since the soil only yields life in the presence of moisture. Moisture is the mysterious element which enables soil to produce the initial phase of every manifestation of life. It is moisture which is found alike in the seed-sprouting rain and in the sperm of animals; the same element—in underground streams, in creeks, in rivers and in oceans, and in the rain—maintains the life of plants, animals and men. The circulation of water in nature is reproduced on a miniature scale in the circulation of the blood in every living organism.

On the Father of Life. . . SUN. Without sun, life on this planet would be impossible. It is by virtue of the sun's rays that the manifold and mysterious processes of life begin or continue in the various plants and trees. Solar energy not only influences but determines the life of all animals and men. It is the sun that creates the temperature favorable to life: above or below certain limits of temperature all manifestations of life on the earth will inevitably be destroyed. It is variations in the intensity of the flow of solar energy which create day and night, and the seasons of the year. The sun is the great force which governs all manifestations of life, the beginning and growth and end of all plants and animals.

On the Breath of Life. . . AIR. The air is charged with all the vital energies which create and sustain life: when we breathe we bring into our bodies all the energies of the atmosphere. "Where is Breath, there is life. Where is Life, there is Breath. Breathing is Life." Breathing is the most universal and indispensable attribute of life, a precondition of every living being. According to the Zend Avesta, the only region on the surface of this planet to possess the preconditions of life is the zone of the earth's atmosphere. Above or below this belt, life is impossible. Breathing is the greatest source of energy. The air is the most rapid bearer of life, and the human body is the possessor of a perfect receiving apparatus for the absorption and instant utilization of the vast sources of energy contained in the vital elements which constitute the earth's atmosphere.

On the Fire of Life. . . VITALITY. Fire is the symbol of purity, and vitality is the purity of the organism. We should feed the "Fire of Life" every day with only pure ingredients, even as we feed the fire on the hearth with dry wood and not with rubbish if we wish to maintain a pure and smokeless flame. We should feed the Fire of Life only with pure and natural foods which are the preconditions of human vitality. Only living, vital foods can nourish the vital processes of the organism to maintain the purity of the Fire of Life.

On Brother Tree and the Food of Life... THE TREE is the most perfect form of life in the vegetable kingdom, and likewise the highest degree of evolution attained in the animal kingdom is represented by man. The highest form of food on this planet is the product of trees—their fruits—and man, as the highest in the animal kingdom, should be nourished by such food. The symbiosis of man and trees furnishes the most harmonious environment for human health and longevity.

"A tree is the Law itself.". . . the life of a tree is in complete harmony with the forces and laws of nature. The life of a tree is the most perfect natural manifestation of life itself. Besides yielding the most perfect food for man, trees maintain the fertility and vitality of the soil; they protect the earth from desiccation by sun and wind; they preserve the life-giving moisture of the top soil with their periodic carpet of fallen leaves and fruit; their roots drain away any excess of humidity and thereby maintain the perfect condition of life—a rich and healthy soil. The tree is the brother of man, and it is a crime to cut down a tree without planting at least two others in its place.

On the Master of Life... MAN. Man is as much a part of nature as are animals or plants, but is indeed a much more important part because in man nature becomes conscious. Thus man is able not only to observe the laws of nature and to live in conformity with them, but also to transform this planet in accordance with these laws. Man represents God on this planet, and continues the work of creation. Before the appearance of man, the planet's evolution was the product of the interplay of the natural forces. Since his coming, man has transformed planetary life by altering it according to his understanding of the natural and cosmic laws. Man is thereby provided with a lofty moral code of marvelous simplicity, a code not only moral but practical, which expresses the quintessence of the natural and cosmic laws and at the same time calls for a system and way of life in accord with man's creative destiny: "Good thoughts, good words, good deeds." This not only proclaims a way of life for the individual, but also regulates the complex relationship between one individual and another, between the individual and the family, between the family and the nation, and between the nation and its leaders. By observance of these precepts—good thoughts, good words, good deeds—man shall continue the work of creation on this planet. This moral code is man's title of nobility and makes it possible for him to perform his glorious role as the dominant species upon the earth.

On the Light of Life. . . WISDOM. Our life is not only determined by what we think, say or do, but also and in greater degree by the thoughts, words, deeds and inventions of the long line of our ancestors representing the sum of all preceding generations whose traditions form the basis of our present life. The totality of riches transmitted to us by previous generations is the "Light of Life."

This light comes to us continually from the most distant ages, making it possible for us to possess the total wisdom and experience of previous generations. We should honor the "Light of Life" represented by the sum of the values of all the great masterpieces of all ages and all nations, by studying them, meditating upon them and trying to translate them into the lives of the individual and society. The greatest fault we can be guilty of is to neglect this "Light of Life" and limit it to only a few rays, instead of absorbing it in its fullness.

On Eternal Life. . . LIFE is not the exclusive privilege of this planet; there are innumerable planets and solar systems in infinite cosmic space where life exists in a wide range of forms. Life is a form of cosmic energy which will always appear wherever favorable preconditions exist. Life is a cosmic function, an inherent quality of the universe, and there is in boundless space and time, a universal solidarity connecting all forms of life on whatever planet. Certain planets or solar systems may disappear or appear, and the life on them likewise, but life itself appearing and disappearing on eternally changing planets and solar systems is as eternal as the universe. And man is a part of this eternal life—of this universal cosmic ocean of life formed by the sum total of all forms of life on all the planets.

Dr. Szekely teaching the Art of Asha. (1979)

"O Man! Why dost thou always wish for something that is not? As the sun is setting, look around thee. . . as the noise and clamor of men fade into deepening dusk. . . see that things *are as they are.* All that is, is just as it should be, and things eternal are exactly *where they are.*"

—The Art of Asha, 1966 *(audio version)*

Stylized Man composed of Rectangle (Power),
Circle (Wisdom), Triangle (Love),
Moon (Peace), Flower (Joy)—Tibet.

Individual Inventory

and Self Analysis

Thousands of years ago, in ancient Sumeria, a system of psychoanalysis was practiced which was much more all-sided than psychoanalysis as practiced today. It is remote from us in time but has a universal quality that modern psychotherapy lacks.

It represents a personal inventory of ideals of conduct and individual evolution, and can be of the greatest value to contemporary man as a balance sheet of his degree of harmony with the Law.

Zarathustra, considering that man lives in the midst of a field of forces, knew that the natural and cosmic forces which surround him and flow through him are superior, positive forces. But he also knew that man by his deviations from the Law in thinking, feeling and acting, constantly creates negative, inferior forces in the midst of which he also lives. He is connected with all of these forces and cannot be separated from them; moreover he is always cooperating, consciously or unconsciously with the superior forces or with the inferior ones. He cannot be neutral.

Under this system, the individual made a weekly self-analysis of his thoughts, words and deeds. This balancing showed the extent to which he was cooperating with or deviating from the superior forces, and gave a cross-section of his character, abilities and physical condition, thus indicating the degree of his evolution in life.

The analysis enabled him to recognize his strong and weak points. By sincerely and vigorously striving to make his thinking, feeling and actions ever better and better, he progressed with the lifetime job of self-improvement.

There may be some who feel that with all the modern

sciences it is unnecessary to go back eight thousand years to an ancient teaching. But it is a question how much the developments of science have accomplished in increasing human happiness and well-being. The general insecurity and neurosis of the present day and the widespread economic and social unrest give a definitely negative answer. Man has gained an enormous amount of theoretical knowledge in the framework of his scientific culture but this has not increased his happiness or individual evolution. It has not served to connect him with the universe, the cosmic order, or to show him his place and role in it.

Without such knowledge man cannot follow the path of optimal evolution for himself or for the planet.

The present-day neurosis is caused by man's current deviations from the law of harmony with natural and cosmic forces. One who tries his best to live in harmony with them will never develop neurosis.

Psychology today tends to emphasize only one or two of these natural forces. Freud, for instance, considered deviations from the law of the natural force of sex caused man's inharmony; others have concentrated on other forms of deviation. But the system practiced in Zarathustra's time considered harmony with all the natural and cosmic forces to be necessary for all-around health and psychological balance. Its superiority over other systems rests in its all-sidedness and universality.

The job of self-improvement, it shows, has to be carried on day by day, by the individual himself. Psychoanalysis, on the other hand, depends largely on the analyst, for the person being analyzed assumes a somewhat passive role. In the Zarathustrian method the achievement of harmony is the lifetime task of the individual, not someone else's job to be completed in a couple of years or less.

The sixteen elements used in the system embrace every aspect of human life. It was not the purpose to divide the natural and cosmic forces into any rigid or artificial pattern, but simply to consider them in such ways as would express most clearly their value and utilization in life.

Perfection was not demanded in the analysis, but the individual was urged to strive continually to improve his relationship to each of the sixteen forces and to achieve ever greater harmony and utilization of their powers and energies. The individual who does this will enjoy an actively creative life, bringing him the highest measure of happiness and service to others. The one who continues to deviate will find life becoming less and less interesting and rewarding, while misery and frustration will become increasingly great.

The World Picture of Zarathustra and the sixteen natural and cosmic forces of ASHA gave man a clear knowledge of his place and role in the universe, and this ancient method of weekly self-analysis enabled him to know how clearly he understood the teaching and how thoroughly he was practicing it, absorbing more and more from these ever present sources of energy, harmony, and knowledge, and following the path of his individual evolution.

Symbol of Ahura Mazda with stylized Zarathustra
or Mazdean Priest in center

Two Mazdean Priests with Stylized Wheel of Eternal Life

Questionnaire

for the Individual Inventory

Each of the sixteen items in the questionnaire is to be considered from three aspects. First: Is the power or force thoroughly *understood?* Second: Does the individual *feel* the importance and significance of it deeply and sincerely? Third: Is the power or force *used* continually?

I.   **SUN**   The sun is a very important source of energy which we should utilize to the utmost.

> a)   Do you understand completely the function of solar energy in the organism?
>
> b)   Do you know in what way you can contact and utilize this energy?
>
> c)   Do you utilize it in the form that is best for your health and well-being?

II.   **WATER**   Everyone should have a bath each morning and use water in the optimal way in diet.

> a)   Do you understand the influence and effect of water upon your health?
>
> b)   Do you feel deeply the role of water in your life?
>
> c)   Do you utilize water in the most efficient ways and do you bathe in water every day of the year?

III.   **AIR**   The importance of spending as much time as possible outdoors and of breathing fresh air.

> a)   Do you know the role of air in life and its effects on the body?
>
> b)   Do you feel deeply the need of pure air and of right breathing?
>
> c)   What practical measures do you take to utilize the energy of the atmosphere for your health?

IV.   **FOOD**   Food of the right kind and in the right amount supplies another vital force of the human organism.

a) Do you know the influence and effect of food on your health? And do you know what are the best foods for the human organism?

b) Do you feel deeply the importance of the right food for your own well-being?

c) Do you utilize this knowledge in the best way, and do you practice what you know continually?

V. **MAN** This represents each person's duty toward one's own individual evolution. We have to try to utilize every moment to further our progress in life, and it is a job which no one can do for us. Nobody and nothing can relieve a human being of this right and responsibility.

a) Do you know and understand all your potentialities and do you know the most practical way of transforming them into reality?

b) Do you feel deeply the importance and necessity of developing your latent capacities?

c) What are you actually doing to bring out the inner aptitudes you have and to develop them to the highest extent so that you may progress little by little in your individual evolution?

VI. **EARTH** Earth represents two aspects of generative force: that which creates life from the soil in the shape of plants, trees, grass and flowers; and that in the human organism which manifests itself in sexual life. Both aspects of generative power create more abundant life on this planet.

1. a) Do you know the best and most practical way of growing plants and food, and the importance of so doing for your own health and the well-being of mankind?

b) Do you feel deeply the urge to grow things and the need for so doing?

c) Do you in fact grow things and make every effort to get the opportunity to do so?

2. a) Do you understand what are the optimal ways of harmonious sexual life and do you realize its importance for your physical and mental health?
    b) Do you feel this deeply within you?
    c) Do you practice complete harmony with and obedience to the Law in this respect?

VII. **HEALTH**   This signifies our relationship to all preceding forces: Sun, Water, Air, Food, Man and Earth, as well as the following one, Joy; for harmony with all of these is necessary for optimal health.

a) Do you realize and understand the importance of good health and of thinking, feeling and acting in the ways most conducive to physical, mental and emotional health?

b) Do you feel deeply the need for health for your own sake and for the sake of others?

c) What are you actually doing to improve your health in respect to all the physical, mental and emotional factors which influence it?

VIII. **JOY**   It is our essential duty and right to be joyous at all times, and when we are in the service of the Law we are always joyous and happy. Sadness and joy have a deep influence on those around us; both are contagious emotions. It is therefore of utmost importance that we should radiate joy at all times.

a) Do you understand the importance of joy in life, and on the health and happiness of those around you?

b) Do you feel the joy of living surging within you continually and do you feel its creative force radiating around you?

c) Do you perform all your daily activities with deep feelings of joy, and do you try to spread this joy around you?

These eight groups of questions represent the visible forces of Nature. The following eight questions concern the invisible powers of the Cosmos, which are even more important. We live in the midst of these cosmic powers and natural forces, and we cannot separate ourselves from them even for an instant. This is why it is so essential that we shall strive continually to create a positive attitude and live in harmony with all of them.

IX. **POWER** Power is manifested continually through our actions and deeds. These are the results of our cooperation with all the other powers and forces in accordance with the iron law of cause and effect. We can perform good deeds only when we are in harmony with all the other laws.

a) Do you understand the importance of good deeds and that your personality, position and environment in life is the result of your past deeds, and that your future will be exactly what your present deeds make it?

b) Do you feel deeply the necessity of performing good deeds at all times and do you consider it a right as well as a duty?

c) Do you actually perform good deeds, and do they express harmony with all the laws of nature and the Cosmos?

X. **LOVE** Love is manifested in the form of good words, for words reveal our attitude to other people. If we feel love toward others, we will speak only gentle and kind words.

a) Do you understand the importance of good words in your own health and emotional life, and for the health and well-being of your fellow man?

b) Do you feel love for all beings around you?

c) Do you practice this diet of harmonious feelings and words towards all beings at all times?

XI. **WISDOM** This represents our duty to increase our knowledge and understanding in every possible way, and to utilize every source of knowledge so that we may improve not only its quantity, but also its quality Wisdom is manifested in the form of good thoughts. Someone may be clever and have a great store of knowledge, but without good thoughts there cannot be wisdom.

> a) Do you understand the extreme importance of a good diet in thoughts for your own health? And do you understand the value of increasing your wisdom so that you may always have good thoughts?
>
> b) Do you long for true wisdom with a deep inner urge?
>
> c) Do you grasp every opportunity to advance and grow in wisdom so as to understand more and more the Cosmic Order and your role in it? And do you hold only good thoughts in your consciousness and refuse even to entertain negative, destructive thoughts about any person, place, condition or thing?

XII. **PRESERVATION OF VALUES** This power concerns the preservation of all useful things and good values, and forms the basis of ecology on our planet. When anyone destroys a good thing or lets it be spoiled or damaged, he is cooperating with the negative, destructive forces of the world. We must use every opportunity to prevent damage to whatever has value, whether a tree, plant, house, relationship between people, or harmony in any form.

> a) Do you realize the importance of preserving all good things, both material and immaterial?
>
> b) Do you feel deeply the need to conserve everything possible and to let nothing deteriorate or go to waste?

c) Do you practice conservation in every way possible and at all times?

XIII. **CREATION**   This signifies the necessity for us to utilize our creative powers: our role on this planet is to continue the work of the Creator. We must therefore try to do something original and creative, something new and different, as often as we can. Every invitation to the Creator to work with and within us, strengthens our creative power.

a) Do you understand the importance of doing or making something creative or original so that you may truly cooperate with the Creator?

b) Do you feel deeply the need for doing something creative and realize the inner satisfaction that results from it?

c) What do you actually do that is original and creative?

XIV. **ETERNAL LIFE**   This concerns our sincerity in all we do and with all those we meet. It concerns also our sincerity with ourselves and in answering all the questions of this questionnaire.

a) Do you understand the necessity of being sincere with all people, including yourself?

b) Do you feel a deep sincerity in analyzing your relationship with all the sixteen forces and powers of Nature and the Cosmos?

c) Can you accept yourself as you are, without rationalizing to justify things you are doing, saying, or thinking?

XV. **WORK**   Work is the precondition of many other values. Work means, among other things, the performance of whatever our daily tasks may be with honesty and efficiency. Work is our contribution to society and is a precondition of happiness for all concerned. For when one person does not perform his work properly, others have to do it.

a) Do you realize the importance of work and the necessity of doing your particular work with care and sincerity, both for your own sake and for that of your social environment?
b) Do you have a deep feeling of satisfaction in your work?
c) Do you do all your daily tasks efficiently and conscientiously and so return to society all you receive from it?

XVI. **PEACE** It is our function and duty first of all to create inner peace and maintain it within ourselves, and then to create and maintain it around us. We should never lose an opportunity to establish peace wherever we find it lacking. If we do this in our environment, and within ourselves, we will be helping to prevent inharmony, enmity and wars, since the condition of the whole of humanity depends upon the condition of its atoms—individual human beings.

a) Do you realize the importance of peace, both within and around you, for the maintenance of your own health and happiness, and that of others?
b) Do you feel deeply the need for this inner peace?
c) Do you actually possess this inner peace and are you trying to do all you can to maintain it within yourself and to establish and maintain it wherever you are?

Zarathustra offering Haoma (Prototype of Mazdean Priest)

The Individual Inventory

MEDITATIONS OF A DISCIPLE

SUN *the reflection of Power*

I try every day to take a short sun bath, knowing that the sun improves the tonus of my skin, creates Vitamin D in my organism, and lulls my nerves into beautiful relaxation. I feel the life-giving energy of the sun enter my body. I am aware that to use this force in the optimal way it is important to have just the right amount of sun: it can be either my best friend or my worst enemy. But when I use it correctly, my body, mind and soul open in joyful thanksgiving for the gift of life.

WATER *the reflection of Love*

In the morning, as soon as possible after awakening, I bathe in clear, fresh water, following one of the primal instincts of Nature for cleanliness. In the splash of a shower, the warmth of a bath, or the refreshment of a dip in an icy stream, water invigorates, cleanses, purifies. I understand the necessity of water to the earth; how barren deserts are turned into beautiful forests only through water, and I have rejoiced to see little birds splashing happily in rain puddles. This same thirst of Nature is present in my body, and I try always to use water—in eating, drinking and bathing—in its freshest, purest form.

AIR *the reflection of Wisdom*

There was a time when I did not think of what kind of air I breathed—only that I did breathe. It did not disturb me that in smoke-filled rooms, in streets full of car exhaust and on smoggy days, my lungs, for protection, took in only the tiniest amount of air necessary for existence. Now that

I know the tremendous importance of deep breathing of pure, fresh air to every one of my physical, mental and spiritual functions, I try at every opportunity to surround myself with pure air, Nature's most important food. Truly is it said, "Where there is breath, there is life; where there is life, there is breath." I am breathing 10,000 quarts of air daily, and my lungs will only be used to their natural, full capacity if the air I am breathing is free of impurities and smoke. Knowing that my mind and body will not develop without the nourishment of pure air, I try to be just as careful of the air I breathe as I am about my food being free of dirt.

FOOD *the reflection of the Preserver*

The cells of my body are made of what I eat; therefore, if I wish to be strong and healthy, I must make sure my body is built from the building blocks of Nature—wholesome, natural foods: proteins without saturated or animal fats; germinated whole grains and sprouts; vegetables, mostly raw in delicious salads; fruits, as they are from trees and vines; honey and dried fruits for energy. Foods which have been refined, preserved through chemicals and overcooked are empty foods, and though they may please an artificially developed taste, they can only deplete my body and rob it of its natural resistance. Therefore, I try my best to give my body only those foods which are as close as possible to their original, natural state.

MAN *the reflection of the Creator*

I know that the primary role of my life is to continue the work of creation on earth. I know that in some unique way I have something original to contribute to the good of society, be it in music, science, art, literature, or education. No matter if my talents are large or small, unusual or prosaic, I must try to discover my hidden potential and use it actively to creatively enrich the world wherein I live. Only in untiring efforts to further my progress in life can I truly find fulfillment as a human being, and I know that no one can do the job for me. Sometimes the realization that only the individual efforts of man, including myself, can change the world for the better, is frightening and awesome; still I know that this most glorious challenge of all is within my power, and my diligent efforts to continue the work of creation will not go unrewarded.

EARTH *the reflection of Eternal Life*
Reproduction, in its many forms, is one of Nature's greatest miracles, and I must learn to respect it, learn from it, and live in harmony with it. In vegetation, especially the wonder of grass, which blankets the earth with the magic of growth, I will learn many secrets of Nature, and I will try to keep a small garden for this purpose. Even if it is just a window box, this attempt at growing things teaches me about many aspects of reproduction. In my body, I know that sexual energy may be used harmoniously to raise a family in accordance with the laws of power, love and wisdom, and this energy may also be used to regenerate the body and find an outlet in the creation of beautiful works of art, literature or music. Whether I decide to use sexual energy for reproduction or regeneration, the important thing is that I use it wisely and harmoniously.

HEALTH *the reflection of Creative Work*
I want more than anything else to be healthy, for I know that only if my body is healthy can I be an active point in the Universe, working to further my own evolution and the evolution of society. Perfect health consists of cooperation with all the natural forces: sun, water, air, food, man, earth

and joy; also, good health rests in balance and moderation: I know that I need exercise to maintain good circulation; I also need plenty of sleep to "recharge my batteries" and renew my energies. A good diet of thoughts and emotions aids my digestion of food, so it is equally important for my health that I cooperate with the cosmic forces as well.

JOY *the reflection of Peace*

Although it is sometimes difficult, I try very hard to be joyous at all times, for I know how great is my power to influence those around me. When I am sad, it does no good to pretend—I sadden those around me, turning their happy moods into bad ones, affecting their nervous systems and even their digestions. When I am happy, I bring as if into a magic circle those around me into my happiness, watching them go away with new courage and strength. When I have negative feelings, I try to think of them as a contagious disease, with which I do not want to infect others. And I know, deep inside, that charity, sermons and good deeds mean very little unless I can give to my fellow man the gift of my own happiness. And what do I need to become happy? Simply the understanding and awareness that life is a precious gift, a privilege that is not to be wasted. As Epictetus said, it is not the things around us that make us happy or unhappy, but only our attitude toward those things. Therefore, I shall continue trying to radiate joy wherever I go, for the world desperately needs it as never before in history.

POWER *the mirror of Sun*

In the Bible it is written, "By their fruits ye shall know them," and I know that unless the private universe of my thoughts and emotions gives birth to good deeds and noble actions, my purpose as co-worker with the Creator is not being fulfilled. Stendahl said, "One can acquire everything in solitude–except character." In the language of Zarathustra, solitude is the silent realm where thought and feeling flow together in their own rhythm of music and fire. But all the beauty of mind and soul are useless unless they are translated into action–action to eliminate human suffering, action to work for the betterment of the human race and the planet on which we live. The present chaos, constant wars and environmental destruction can never be controlled by peaceful attitudes alone: action is needed, *my* action, not someone else's. I know I do not need to travel across the world to crusade against evil–my family, my friends, my place of work, all provide me with a vast arena where I may slay innumerable dragons of ignorance, injustice, intolerance and disharmony in many forms. Zarathustra writes in the Zend Avesta, "Evil exists not, only the past; the past is past, the present is a moment, the future is all." Only by my good deeds and actions in the present can I mold the future of which Zarathustra spoke.

LOVE *the mirror of Water*
Just as the force of Power is manifested in deeds, so is the force of Love expressed in words. I know that until I have attained psychological maturity, it will be impossible to love every person I meet in life with wisdom and detachment, but by learning to allow only loving words to express my thoughts, I can actively cooperate with the force of Love, and better my own life and the lives of those I come in contact with. Love is unity; in the Cosmic Ocean of Love all forms of life are united–life itself is an expression of love. Therefore I remind myself each day that it is not important whether I agree with, disagree with, approve of, or disapprove of my fellow man. The main thing is that we

are all cells of one body, the Cosmic Ocean, and a growing awareness of this basic oneness will more than anything else develop my ability to love. I try to follow the counsel of Buddha, who advised that each time before speaking we ask ourselves three questions: *"Is it true, is it needful, is it kind?"*

WISDOM *the mirror of Air*

To always have good thoughts is the essence of Wisdom, but oh, how much more difficult it is than to say good words and do good deeds! For words and deeds may be controlled through discipline, but thoughts have a way of entering unbidden and departing without leave, and I realize that until I can rein in the wild horses of my thoughts, I am no better than a slave in a harshly ruled country. So I try and try, and keep trying. Knowing that two things cannot exist in the same place at the same time, my strongest weapon is to strengthen the good in all I encounter, instead of trying to fight the evil. By trying to let only harmonious thoughts enter my mind, I am refusing to give reality to negative, destructive thoughts. Thoughts are immensely powerful vibrations, and it is up to me to create heaven or hell for myself and others, depending on the quality of my thoughts. When temptation arrives in the form of depression, despair or sadness, I try to "tune in" to the thoughts of the great masters, philosophers, musicians, artists and poets of history, feeling their ageless power rescue me from the mediocre and banal thoughts of all those who live lives of "ignorance in action." In the Zend Avesta it is written, "In what fashion is manifest Thy Law? O Thou Great Creator! By good thought in perfect unity with reason, O Zarathustra!" By always seeking out the wise, the good, and the beautiful, I will gradually learn to conquer my thoughts. Until I do, it is of no use to conquer anything else.

THE PRESERVER *the mirror of Food*

In my efforts to understand and cooperate with the law of preservation, I realize more and more why the Preserver on the board of Asha has more power and versatility than any other figure. All that has been created, everything of beauty, everything of value must be steadily guarded and maintained, or the act of creation has no significance. Michelangelo's paintings in the Sistine Chapel are precious beyond any price and enrich the spiritual lives of millions; yet a careless bomb in a needless war could destroy it in seconds. A friendship is not a static thing but a dynamic, changing relationship, and a reckless word may damage it beyond repair. Every species of wild creature that vanishes takes a part of our souls into oblivion. Friendship, love, works of art, untouched wilderness, whatever the creation, the word has no meaning without preservation. Sometimes I am helpless to prevent waste and destruction, as in the case of war; yet in my own sphere of activity I can use my influence in countless ways to help protect, preserve, and practice prevention; grass, trees, flowers, a house, the trust of a child, whatever it may be, material or immaterial, the act of Preservation is the indispensable twin of Creation. Every time I cooperate with the Preserver, I hear anew the words of the Zend Avesta: "The Keepers and Preservers of the Earth shall restore the World! When Life and Immortality will come and Creation will grow deathless!"

THE CREATOR *the mirror of Man*

I am told that my role on this planet is to continue the work of the Creator. Immense and awesome and nearly impossible does this role seem to me, for I am not a Beethoven, a Shakespeare, nor a Leonardo da Vinci. Nevertheless, by utilizing whatever small talents I may have and struggling to uncover my hidden potential, I am unconsciously setting in motion my creative powers. After all, on the board of Asha I stand with the Creator directly behind me. If my desire is great and my efforts sincere, no one can predict in what areas and in what paths my creative ability may develop. Again the Zend Avesta: "The Creative Mind within us is causing the Imperishable Kingdom to progress." From these words I know that the Creative Mind is slumbering within, waiting to be awakened through incessant striving. As long as my goal is the Imperishable Kingdom, the realm of Creation may well be mine to rule, explore and obey.

ETERNAL LIFE *the mirror of Earth*
This is the only force that assails me with unanswerable questions: What exactly does Eternal Life mean? Is it the perpetuation of my species or my own personal eternity? If I am to live forever, why do I not remember having lived before? And so on, and on. Though my immature need of security will continue to ask, the answer of the Zend Avesta is simple: "Let the enlightened alone speak to the enlightened." In other words, metaphysical speculations about Eternal Life are irrelevant; to cooperate with this force means that I must live my life eternally, here and now, as if each day were my last, savoring every precious moment, utilizing each minute of every day to help eliminate human suffering and teach others through example. It was Goethe who said, "To reach the infinite, one must tread the finite in every direction." To understand Eternal Life, I must first understand everything about this life; instead of asking futile questions about what happens when I die, I will make my own eternity in the present, by accepting myself as I am without rationalization, by approaching all my tasks with sincerity and honesty, and not shirking my responsibilities. ". . .and the same inexorable price must still be paid for the same great purchase. . ." The

price of Eternal Life is sincerity, honesty and incessant striving in this one.

WORK *the mirror of Health*

Those who consider work as a hardship and a burden will never be able to understand this force. "Only a select few can rise to the conception of work as the supreme realization of the mind." How the numbers of that "select few" would swell if all people could experience the joy and radiance of creative work! "Happy is the one who has found his task; he should not ask for any other blessing." Only through work am I able to put into practice the principles of power, love, wisdom, peace and joy; only in work can I move among men and teach the things I have learned. The one who complains about the nature of his work complains without reason; if the will and desire are strong enough, any kind of work will reflect the Law, and even the lofty roles of Teacher and Priest are worth only as much as they are in harmony with the Law. When I feel gratitude and love surge within me for the gift of life and the pursuit of knowledge, I know that only work done well can prove the sincerity of my feelings. The Zend Avesta: "What is Thy Kingdom, O Creator? What are Thy riches? Thine Own, in my Work, in my Holy Service."

PEACE *the mirror of Joy*

I know that deep, lasting peace within myself can come only when I live in true harmony with all the sixteen natural and cosmic forces. It is the result, the crown, the golden aura that surrounds the mountain of hard work and striving. Still, as I tread the path of daily effort, there will be many opportunities for me to either contribute to the cause of peace or to that of discord; a simple word, a gesture, a calm judgment may bring communication where there was a lack of it; settle an argument that would have swelled and multiplied; or bring harmony into an atmosphere usually devoid of it. People who constantly live on the sharp edge of nervous tension and anxiety are slowly being poisoned by their emotions. My peaceful efforts to soothe, calm and relax are balm more important than pills or potions. My own Peace, solemn and mysterious, may only be at present a whisper of the future; yet I can give what I have. . . peace to answer the chaos around me, peace to still the frantic clamor of those who seek security in material things, peace to strengthen the spirit of those who desperately want to find their Home but know not how. I feel very certain that though I am but a pilgrim and I make many mistakes, the very act of trying to understand these sixteen forces, of feeling their power in my life, of making my actions manifest their purposes, gives me the power to guide, direct and teach in a way I never would have thought possible. This is my peace. . . even before reaching my goal. . . of being on the Path, and knowing that to travel this Path hopefully and joyously is my glorious mission and the mission of all mankind.

Norma teaching the Art of Asha. (1984)

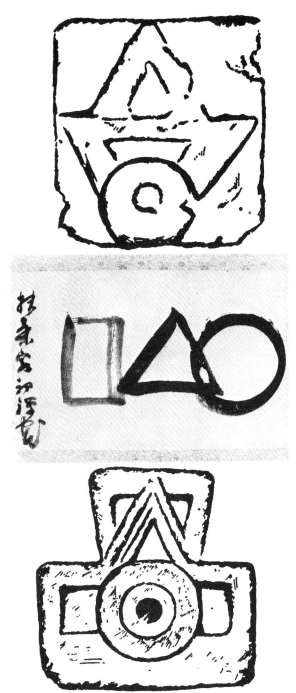

(top and bottom) Designs from ancient Sumeria using symbols of the Creator, Power, Love and Wisdom. (center) Symbol of the Universe (Power, Love, Wisdom), by Sengai, Edo period, Japan.

Journey to the Cosmic Ocean and

Individual Fulfillment

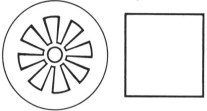

SUN . . . POWER . . . rays of golden, vital
energy penetrate our solar center, awakening
all that is sleeping and dormant . . . the song
of growth is heard in the soil, leaves turn green
and flowers open . . . "Of all flowers it is the
human flower which has most need of sun" . . .
the sun brings life to earth . . . Power manifested
in deeds brings the life of the spirit to man . . .
Good Thoughts and Good Words find their
outlet in Good Deeds . . . and in the Mirror of
the Cosmic Ocean of Life, the rays of Sun and
Power meet in the acting body of Man. . . .

WATER ... LOVE ... *drops of tender rain on*
thirsty earth ... swallows drink gratefully
from a mountain pond ... the body of man is
washed clean of the dust and grime of toil ...
rivers, oceans, lakes and seas ... the circulation
of the blood, carrying the water of life to the
body ... water quenches the thirst of the earth
as love soothes the pain of the feeling body ...
separation, loneliness ... only Love can make
smooth the sharp edge of suffering ... as we
love, so do we learn to love more ... life itself
is an expression of love ... the Cosmic Ocean
of Love exists everywhere uniting all living
beings ... its embrace circles the universe and
in its cool waters is dissolved all the pain
of existence. ...

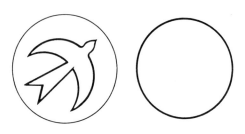

AIR . . . WISDOM . . . an eagle soars through the sky, leaving behind a streak of blue . . . the electric purity of the mountain air seeks the nostrils of man . . . the breath of life . . . the link between Man and the Cosmos . . . the Cosmic Ocean of Thought pervades all space . . . the highest, most powerful of all cosmic energies . . . the true food of man . . . as he breathes deeply, the cells of his body cry out in gratitude . . .and his mind rejoices in the stirrings of abstract thought . . . consciousness of the Law . . . Wisdom . . . the pinnacle of reason . . . to guide the words of love into harmony of action. . . .

FOOD . . . the PRESERVER . . . the sacred fire
of the human body . . .the horn of plenty of
the earth overflows . . . fruits and vegetables,
whole grains and nuts . . . all has been provided
. . . there is no need for lifeless substitutes . . .
to preserve the body we need only to feast at
the table of Nature . . . to preserve the values
of love, friendship, honor and loyalty, we must
ever be alert . . . to protect a tree, a house, a
plot of grass . . . no effort is too small . . . for
to create is to join hands with the Creator . . .
to preserve is to walk with Him forever. . . .

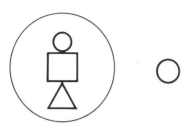

MAN . . . the CREATOR . . . Mystery of
mysteries . . . the Hand of the Creator on the
forehead of Man . . . urging him to continue
the work of Creation . . . Man, the chosen . . .
yet he must choose . . . his talents, his abilities,
his potential . . . whether they remain dreams
or become realities . . . all depends on Man . . .
the glorious, awesome, impossible, inevitable
task of continuing the work of Creation on
the planet called Earth. . . .

EARTH... *ETERNAL LIFE... in the darkness*
of the womb a child is conceived... in the
darkness of the soil a seed becomes a flower...
in the night of the spirit a soul is born which
shall never die... nothing is lost in the universe
... the mirror of Eternal Life has a side visible
to Man... the bright surface of Sincerity...
acceptance of oneself without rationalization
... honesty in attitudes... sincere examination
of faults... on this difficult path is the other
side of the mirror of Eternal Life reached
... and surpassed....

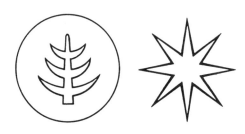

HEALTH . . . WORK . . . *the cleansing aroma*
of activity . . . to feel the very blood move
faster . . . to know the keen pleasure of deserved
weariness . . . "To love is to go on teaching
forever without becoming weary" . . . to watch
the flash of recognition in the eyes of another
. . . a thought, an idea communicated . . . to be
submerged in a task that is beyond the ordinary
days of those who do not know . . . to be healthy
is to work . . . to work is to be healthy . . .
there is no other way open to thee, o man,
save the way of work. . . .

JOY . . . PEACE . . . *the warmth of joy radiates out, to those passing by . . . a smile travels, reaches its destination, warms and gladdens . . . joy cannot be contained . . . effervescent bubbles escape and tickle . . . and laughter begins . . . and a small portion of frightened, lonely humanity is helped back to the wide road . . . it is a crime not to love life . . . the laughing Spring of Joy beckons to the golden Autumn of Peace . . . a gentle hand of serenity that takes no notice of the chaos around it . . . a gentleness within . . . that seeks its own in the outside world but finds it not . . . no matter . . . Peace dwells in patience . . . and waits. . . .*

Stylized Man composed of Square (Power), Circle (Wisdom),
Triangle (Love), Moon (Peace), Flower (Joy) — Chinese

BIBLIOGRAPHY & REFERENCES

ANQUETIL-DUPERRON
Zend Avesta, Ouvrage de Zoroastre, 3 vols. 1771

J. DARMESTETER
Le Zendavesta 1879 & Ormuzd et Ahriman 1883

MAX MULLER
Persische Literatur

M. HAUG
*Essays on the Sacred Language and Religion
of the Parsis 1884*

N. BLAND
Persian Chess 1850

K. GELDNER
Grundriss der Iranischen Philologie 1896

SIR JOHN MARSHALL
The Cuneiform Symbols of Sumeria

F. WOLF
Avesta 1910

EDMOND BORDEAUX SZEKELY
*The Zend Avesta of Zarathustra
The Essene Teachings of Zarathustra
Archeosophy, a New Science*

ACKNOWLEDGEMENT*

I would like to express my sincerest appreciation to Miss Norma Jean Nilsson for her excellent adaptation of materials from one of my previously published books, "The World Picture of Zarathustra," and for her thorough editing of this book. I also want to thank Miss Vivian Blackstone for her excellent art work and for her adaptation of illustrations from the same "World Picture of Zarathustra." Without the help of my two collaborators the publication of this book would not have been possible.

The Author

*from the original 1966 edition.

FOOD   MAN   EARTH   HEALTH

ESERVER   CREATOR   ETERNAL   WO
                        LIFE

Norma continues the Art of Asha. . .

CREDO
of the International Biogenic Society

We believe that our most precious possession is Life.

We believe we shall mobilize all the forces of Life against the forces of death.

We believe that mutual understanding leads toward mutual cooperation; that mutual cooperation leads toward Peace; and that Peace is the only way of survival for mankind.

We believe that we shall preserve instead of waste our natural resources, which are the heritage of our children.

We believe that we shall avoid the pollution of our air, water, and soil, the basic preconditions of Life.

We believe we shall preserve the vegetation of our planet; the humble grass which came fifty million years ago, and the majestic trees which came twenty million years ago, to prepare our planet for mankind.

We believe we shall eat only fresh, natural, pure, whole foods, without chemicals and artificial processing.

We believe we shall live a simple, natural, creative life, absorbing all the sources of energy, harmony and knowledge, in and around us.

We believe that the improvement of life and mankind on our planet must start with individual efforts, as the whole depends on the atoms composing it.

We believe in the Fatherhood of God, the Motherhood of Nature, and the Brotherhood of Man.

—composed in Paris in 1928 by Romain Rolland
and Edmond Bordeaux Szekely

THE STORY OF THE ESSENE GOSPEL OF PEACE

Translated by Edmond Bordeaux Szekely

In Four Volumes

It was in 1928 that Edmond Bordeaux Szekely first published his translation of Book One of *The Essene Gospel of Peace*, an ancient manuscript he had found in the Secret Archives of the Vatican as the result of limitless patience, faultless scholarship, and unerring intuition. This story is told in his book *The Discovery of the Essene Gospel of Peace*, published in 1975. The English version of Book One appeared in 1937, and ever since, the little volume has traveled over the world, appearing in many different languages, gaining every year more and more readers, until now, still with no commercial advertisement, over a million copies have been sold in the United States alone. It was not until almost fifty years after the first French translation that Book Two and Book Three appeared *(The Unknown Books of the Essenes* and *Lost Scrolls of the Essene Brotherhood)*, achieving rapidly the popularity of Book One.

In 1981, Book Four, *The Teachings of the Elect*, was published posthumously according to Dr. Szekely's wishes, representing yet another fragment of the complete manuscript which exists in Aramaic in the Secret Archives of the Vatican and in old Slavonic in the Royal Library of the Habsburgs in Austria. The poetic style of the translator brings to vivid reality the exquisitely beautiful words of Jesus and the Elders of the Essene Brotherhood. Some of the chapters: The Essene Communions. The Sevenfold Peace. The Holy Streams of Life, Light, and Sound. The Gift of the Humble Grass.

All four volumes of *The Essene Gospel of Peace* are available in English from the International Biogenic Society, mailing address: I.B.S. Internacional, P.O. Box 849, Nelson, B.C., Canada V1L 6A5. A free descriptive catalogue of these and all the collected works of Edmond Bordeaux Szekely will be gladly sent upon request.

APPLICATION FOR ASSOCIATE MEMBERSHIP
INTERNATIONAL BIOGENIC SOCIETY

Please return to: *I.B.S. Internacional*
        P O Box 849, Nelson, B.C.
        Canada V1L 6A5

*Name*_____

*Address*_____

*City, State/Prov., Zip/Code*_____

*Age*____*Profession*_____

*Previous Experience*_____

I am interested in:

  ____*becoming an Associate Member of the I.B.S.*
  ____*becoming a Teacher of Biogenic Living.*

Enclosed is my annual Associate Membership fee of U.S. $20.00. Please mail me my membership card, your current issue of the Periodical Review, *The Essene Way,* and my copy of *The Essene Way-Biogenic Living,* my "Guidebook," textbook and encyclopedia of ancient wisdom and modern practice. I understand I will receive a 20% discount on all publications as an Associate Member, but only if I order *directly* from I.B.S. Internacional.

Please make your check in U.S. currency out to
I.B.S. INTERNACIONAL.

P.S. The only reason we ask your age, profession and "previous experience" (whatever that means) is just to get to know you a little, as we may never have the chance to meet you personally. If you don't want to answer, it's OK.

RECOMMENDED BOOKS FOR STUDY

Many members who have not yet started study groups or live far from book stores and/or like-minded individuals, are interested in a systematic program of home study. The following books are recommended for such a program, and provide an excellent foundation for study of *The Essene Way of Biogenic Living*, especially when coordinated with the methods outlined in *The Art of Study: the Sorbonne Method.*

Please send me the following books:

___The Essene Gospel of Peace, Book One $1.00

___The Essene Gospel of Peace, Book Two $9.50

___The Essene Gospel of Peace, Book Three $9.50

___The Essene Gospel of Peace, Book Four $7.50

___The Essene Way-Biogenic Living $11.50 (free with membership)

___The Biogenic Revolution $11.95

___The Chemistry of Youth $9.50

___From Enoch to the Dead Sea Scrolls $7.50

___The Essene Book of Creation $5.95

___The Essene Code of Life $4.50

___The Essene Science of Life $4.50

___Essene Communions with the Infinite $5.95

___Discovery of the Essene Gospel of Peace $7.50

___The Essene Book of Asha $9.50

___Books, Our Eternal Companions $4.50

___Cosmos, Man and Society $8.95

___Search for the Ageless, Volume One $10.50

___Search for the Ageless, Volume Two $11.50

___The Ecological Health Garden, the Book of Survival $7.50

___The Art of Study: the Sorbonne Method $4.50

_____Sub-Total

_____Add 15% for Postage & Handling ($3.00 minimum)

U.S. $_____Total Amount Enclosed

I.B.S. INTERNACIONAL
Box 849, Nelson, B.C., Canada V1L 6A5

Name_____

Address_____

City, State/Province, Zip/Code_____

All orders must be pre-paid. Minimum order: $10.00, minimum postage: $3.00 (foreign orders may be more). Please make check, bank draft or money order in U.S. FUNDS, drawn on a U.S. BANK, with the proper "microencoding" at the bottom of the check, out to I.B.S. INTERNACIONAL. Allow at least 4 weeks for processing, more for foreign orders. Members and Teachers of the I.B.S. may apply their usual discounts (both must have valid memberships for the current year). *All sales are considered final; please do not return any books.* If there are any questions, PLEASE WRITE before acting, and please print legibly. Dealers and distributors, write for discount information. All books have always been sent from our warehouse in the U.S., hence the necessity for payment in U.S. funds. Thank you! We send you fraternal greetings and hope to hear from you soon!

128